ISSUE #21 - VIRTUAL PRODUCTION

Motion bases, mo-co cameras and monofilament wires 4
How to ride a dragon 12
Shooting on an LED volume…on film 16
In the volume with gladiators, chariots and horses 30
Getting up to speed with LED walls for indies 46
The virtual tech of 'Ted' 50
Virtual production: a state of play with Jim Geduldick 62
Breaking down a virtual production shoot 70

EDITOR
Ian Failes
beforesandafters@gmail.com

COVER IMAGE
Dragon riding scenes in season 2 of *House of the Dragon* made use of early previs and techvis, a buck on a motion base, a robotic motion-controlled camera, live comps and LED lighting panels. © 2024 HBO.

beforesandafters.com

© 2024 befores & afters

THE INDUSTRY STANDARD
FOR VISUAL EFFECTS
NOW WITH ANIMATED VDB ASSETS

The High-Impact Gas Explosions collection features 20 detailed animated 3D VDB assets, designed to deliver dynamic and powerful visual effects. Each explosion in the collection is crafted to offer versatility and realism, with the ability to rotate and position the effect to match the specific perspective and context of your scene.

  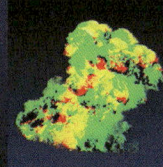 

Compatibility is key for seamless integration into existing workflows, and these 3D explosions are designed to work effortlessly with all major 3D software and render engines that support VDB files.

SCAN ME

MOTION BASES, MO-CO CAMERAS AND MONOFILAMENT WIRES

Behind the techniques used to craft the dragon riding scenes in season two of House of the Dragon. **By Ian Failes.**

The many dramatic dragon riding scenes in season two of HBO's *House of the Dragon* brought audiences incredibly close and upfront with the riders atop their beasts. That required developing a clear methodology for bringing those riding scenes to life.

Several VFX and virtual production-related techniques were therefore overseen by visual effects supervisor Daði Einarsson and visual effects producer Tom Horton—all the way from previs, to shooting actors on a motion base, using a robotic motion control camera, incorporating interactive lighting from LED lighting panels, completing live composites, and even some old-school wind machines and wires during the shoot.

PLANNING THE DRAGON RIDES

"The overall idea was to use previs and take it to a fairly high animation level," Einarsson tells *befores & afters*, in relation to the preparation required to orchestrate the dragon riding scenes. "We actually had finaling animation artists on the previs, because the point of the previs was to get final cameras and final animation in the saddle area in order to be able to techvis that and transpose the camera and the saddle movement onto a motion control Bolt X camera and a multi-axis gimbal buck."

The majority of the dragon riding scenes were previsualized by Pixomondo, which was also responsible for several virtual production services on set, as well as being one of the vendors completing final VFX and animation of the CG dragon sequences. Pixomondo also managed the virtual production on a handful of dragon riding scenes that The Third Floor completed previsualization on.

The process started with creative previs. "We were not worrying at all about the technical side of it," notes Einarsson. "We had quite a specific constraint methodology about what kind of camera work we wanted to use on the dragons. The creative brief was that we wanted to ground the camera work in realism, that is, avoiding magical cameras. We had two basic shooting styles. One of them we called the dragon mounted camera, as if there was a camera operator sitting somewhere on the dragon, say, either on the neck or behind the saddle. We also kept this a little bit loose on the saddle, like it was a handheld shot."

"The other shooting style was dragon to dragon, as if our camera would be mounted on another dragon," continues Einarsson. "We imagined, if this was all real, then the camera work would feel like aerial photography that we are just used to seeing, which grounds our fantasy in a little bit of reality."

Pixomondo's approach to the previs was to give each dragon a unique visual identity in animation, such as distinct wing cadences and heightened performance. "We then applied the detailed animation data to the on-set buck rig," discusses Pixomondo virtual production supervisor James Thompson, "enabling actors to closely mimic the dragons' flight movements, synchronized with a motion-controlled camera for more immersive shots."

Einarsson looked to bring the previs animation about 80% of the way to final. "Obviously you're missing facial and overlap of the wings and the head. But we didn't worry too much about that. We just wanted to get it so that the weight was definitely there with the gross movement of the body. Once you've got it in there, you can always do a little bit of tweaking. You can loosen the camera up a bit and add the final process. For instance, when we took it all the way to final comp, then we'd be sometimes widening the camera a little bit and adding more camera shake and stuff that we didn't want to bake into the motion control."

Pixomondo then re-worked the previs into techvis, which involved creating a 3D virtual scene that replicated the on-set hardware. "The idea here was to select the 3D camera and constrain it to our motion control camera," outlines Einarsson. "You can select the saddle or the saddle constraint of the flying dragon and constrain it in 3D space to the buck. That basically reverse-engineers the movement. It takes out the global movement and puts it into a single space."

Once approved, the techvis data was transferred to the motion control hardware and buck rig for testing. "During this phase," relates Thompson, "shots were tested with stunts and camera crews, and the rushes were sent to the production team for approval. We worked closely with the director of photography and gaffers during pre-lighting to fine-tune the lighting on the LED walls, using a custom Unreal Engine setup for instant feedback."

SHOOTING THE SCENES

The riding buck on which an actor sat for filming was positioned on a four axis motion base. This was orchestrated by special effects supervisor Mike Dawson, with Ian Menzies from Mark Roberts Motion Control handling the control of the motion base. The buck was fitted with an art department-designed saddle.

"We've got an amazing props department, set department and a whole saddle team that built all of these saddles," details Einarsson. "For anything that we are going to shoot a principal cast member on, we'll have the full saddle built. Each one of those saddles is just an amazing design. We built all of the saddles that we needed for the buck work."

Buck shoots for dragon scenes have of course been a part of the *Game of Thrones* and *House of the Dragon* universe for several years. But one of the new approaches included for this season was the addition of the Bolt X robotic motion control camera (supplied by Mark Roberts Motion Control). "What it gave us was the ability to be able to previs the shot design and animate the shot exactly how we wanted it to look," states Einarsson. "If we didn't have motion control cameras, then everything would just have been an estimation. You could eyeball it, but you need to have control over the buck, control over the camera and control over the world lighting. Those three elements allow you to deconstruct a dragon that's flying around in 3D space and shoot it precisely the way you want it framed."

"If we had a Technocrane or something like that, then you're always just eyeballing it," reinforces Einarsson. "You can start slipping into designing the shot on the day or tweaking it or wanting to try a different version of it. The

schedule can go out the window. Plus, it can mean you completely break the methodology of the dragon mounted camera or the dragon to dragon camera. It becomes like a crane around a flying thing. You lose the grounding of camera work that we've become attuned to expect from actual flying scenes like a World War II dogfight, where you've got cameras, cockpit cameras or you've got a plane next to it. That's the film language that we've come to expect from flying scenes."

A further consideration during the buck shoot was adding in atmospheric effects, such as wind, on the actors. "We were trying to replicate them flying at 160 miles an hour, so there had to be quite of lot of wind from wind machines to blow around their capes," notes Einarsson. "We actually had to use monofilaments because the capes would wrap under or get caught in the saddles. So we had these wires that held them out, and then wind machines and handheld windblowers to try and get them to swirl in the right way."

THE APPROACH TO LIGHTING

LED panels were positioned around the buck in an adjustable horseshoe-shaped wall with a ceiling panel. Two panels were also angled toward the horseshoe and mounted on Manitous for quick repositioning if necessary. The panels featured a basic sky and cloud animation, dragon wings and fire. The intention here was interactive lighting, especially to reflect upon the actors' armor. The imagery was all synchronized with the motion-controlled camera and buck rig, an effort crafted by Pixomondo running live through Unreal Engine.

"Although environments from the previs were not used as backgrounds during shooting, the animated CG dragons were displayed on the LED walls to cast realistic moving shadows on actors riding the buck rig," says Thompson.

"Additionally, cloud effects and animated eyeline markers were used to maintain consistent actor focus. Our Unreal system allowed for immediate adjustments to these elements as needed."

This kind of setup was preferred to running a full LED volume. The imagery displayed on the LED panels was also not intended for in-camera 'final pixel' visual effects shots. That would have required generating high-resolution Unreal Engine imagery for an LED wall perfectly in sync with the performances. Einarsson says this would have been a difficult task with so much other production and shooting going on at the same time.

"The amount of dialing in the look of the environment is not very practical to do during production. Then there's changes that might happen in the edit, and you can be stuck with the lighting that you shot, which might be different from what you're cutting around. Just the amount of asset work and tweaking and finding the secret sauce of how to make it look great, that's something you really want to do during post."

"There's also a very big cost involved in creating a photoreal volume," adds Einarsson. "There's a lot of asset work that you need to do up front, and you have to work within a particular schedule. We also have eight executive producers and five directors, so it's almost like making five features at the same time. And, honestly, the chances of replacing a picture-ready background anyway in post are pretty high."

Einarsson notes that a further challenge was that many battles had action occurring both in the air and on the ground simultaneously. "If the whole battle happened in the air, then we'd certainly know exactly what our whole environment is and it wouldn't need to match any other live-action or other environment, then I think there'd be a good argument for it. But for what we did, we were very happy to have a lot of control over the lighting."

THE BENEFIT OF LIVE-COMPS

During the shoot, a blue frustum was able to be projected on the LED panel behind the actor. It enabled a live key to be made of the actor and saddle that could be composited over the previs footage (sans the CG previs actor and CG saddle). Pixomondo built the system to enable this approach.

"During the early shoots," outlines Thompson, "we began developing a system in Unreal Engine that would enable real-time visualization of actors riding on CG dragons. We recognized early on how invaluable this tool would be for both our team and the client on the production side, as it would allow for the validation of VFX shots in real-world conditions. The solved scene in Maya, derived from our previsualization, was designed to be a virtual replication of the hardware and stage setup on set. One of the initial challenges we faced was ensuring that our Unreal scene had an identical rig and stage setup as the physical set. To streamline this process, our developers created tools that would facilitate quick integration between the two software environments."

"Another challenge we encountered early on," says Thompson, "was figuring out how to sync the on-set rigs, controlled by Flair, with our setup in Unreal Engine. To address this, we worked closely with Mark Roberts' team and developed a receiver system that could read various data streams over the network, including frame count, allowing Flair to trigger our system. Although we identified slight delays in receiving this data, we were able to offset these delays, ensuring smooth synchronization between the physical rigs and the virtual scene."

One of the further benefits of both the previs process and the recorded live comps of the dragon riding scenes was that there was then effectively an accurate postvis of the sequences that could go straight into editorial. "Editorial and story-wise, this was very useful, and they could use it directly," comments Einarsson. "In fact, the whole process proved extremely useful in showing everybody a work in progress. The cast could see it in previs, then do the shot, come down and basically see a rough assembly immediately. We could then also give that to our vendors–Pixomondo, Rodeo FX and Wētā FX–for them to complete the final VFX." **b&a**

Page 4: Dragon riding scenes in season 2 of House of the Dragon made use of early previs and techvis, a buck on a motion base, a robotic motion-controlled camera, live comps and LED lighting panels.

Page 7: The final shot by Pixomondo.

Page 8: A Pixomondo previs frame.

Page 11: A final shot by Rodeo FX.

All images © 2024 HBO.

HOW TO RIDE A DRAGON

Pixomondo virtual production supervisor **James Thompson** *breaks down the on-set shoot and the VP methodologies employed for the dragon riding scenes in season 2 of House of the Dragon.*

A typical shoot day for the dragon riding scenes would begin before the official call time, ensuring all the on-set hardware and software was fully operational, synchronized, and ready to go. My first task was to confirm that the team managing the LED wall lighting had their systems properly communicating with the compute hardware running the panels. I also coordinated with Mark Roberts' team to ensure the buck rig and Bolt X were functioning correctly and that we were receiving the necessary frame count data to trigger our real-time system. It was essential to verify that we were receiving video feeds from the DITs and that they had everything they needed to display our real-time visualization in the video village. Additionally, I checked with the on-set 'slap comper' to ensure he had all the elements required for the day's shots, alongside other routine checks, such as confirming the correct timecode synchronization across all systems.

Once I had the day's shot list from VFX production manager Adam Lawrence, I made sure Mark Roberts had the correct moves prep'ed for each shot and that our team handling the lighting and real-time visualization had the relevant data loaded and ready. Throughout the shoot, I was actively involved in managing any necessary adjustments to the motion control, real-time visualization, and LED walls. This could involve facilitating quick animation changes, either directly or through Mark Roberts, in response to the director's requests.

On the real-time visualization side, I worked closely with the team to ensure that the CG elements were properly aligned and synchronized, and to provide playback when needed. Managing the LED walls required constant communication with the director, DOPs, VFX supervisor, and the Pixomondo team to ensure that lighting adjustments met the DOP's requirements. Collaborating with the VFX supervisor and DOP, I made sure the bluescreen on the wall was following the camera's frustum and provided adequate coverage for the actor and the saddle. The DOP would often request additional elements, like fire, which we sourced from our VFX team. Another critical aspect of lighting was creating the appropriate shadows, which involved projecting animated dragon wings on the LED walls. These needed to sync precisely with the cadence of the buck rig animation for a realistic effect, requiring quick offsets and animation adjustments. Our team also created cloud effects that could be adjusted in speed or contrast at the DOP's request.

Ideally, all shots approved during previsualization and testing would be ready to execute, but in practice, flexibility was crucial to maintaining creative freedom during shooting. Often, a shot would look different in pre-production than it did with all elements running together and the actor performing. To accommodate this, we maintained close communication with the director to implement any changes he or she might need, whether in camera movement or buck rig motion. Thanks to a robust workflow and pipeline, we could efficiently make these adjustments without putting undue strain on the shoot schedule. Our camera and rig solving was done in Maya, allowing us to quickly export elements for real-time visualization and lighting into Unreal Engine within minutes.

There were instances where we had to reposition the camera to provide more frame coverage, allowing for additional camera shake in post-production. Communicating with the director about the placement of eyeline markers or bloops on the LED wall was another important task, especially when these markers needed to be animated depending on the shot. Ensuring that the key light on the LED wall was positioned correctly, based on the previsualized scene rather than the physical setup, was essential. This often meant moving the light around the buck rig and rider in perfect sync with the Bolt X. Throughout all of this, I remained in close communication with the VFX supervisor to serve as an extra set of eyes, validating the shot and checking for any potential issues. I also double-checked with the camera team to ensure we were using the correct lens based on what had been signed off during testing.

The on-set setup for these shots included a buck rig (motion base) with a removable top to accommodate different saddles, depending on the dragon being shot. Wind blowers were also fitted to the buck rig. The Bolt X robot was chosen early on as the primary camera tool after extensive deliberation with Mark Roberts' team, taking into account the shot lists and previs. One limitation of the Bolt X was its reach, so for certain shots requiring an overhead perspective, we mounted it on top of a shipping container. This setup provided the necessary reach while retaining the robot's speed advantages. We also devised a method to have the Bolt X follow the buck rig, simulating the effect of the camera being attached to the rig, while still allowing manual control of pan and tilt. This innovation saved significant time in rigging and de-rigging for specific shots.

Our real-time system was built using Unreal Engine, allowing us to control both lighting and elements on the panels within the same environment. This unified setup was crucial for synchronizing all the data. By integrating with the Flair system operated by Mark Roberts' team, we ensured that the start of a move would immediately trigger our sequence in Unreal Engine. Another advantage of this integration was the ability to replicate the world camera position from the Bolt X in our 3D scene.

I believe that the on-set virtual production work we implemented on *House of the Dragon* season 2 offers significant advantages for post-production. The setup we used allowed us to elevate the performance of the actors and enhance the overall feel of the camera work, thanks to the speed and range of movement achievable with the Bolt X camera and buck rig. By incorporating dragon animations from the previs scenes, we provided the post teams with a consistent flight cadence, aligning with the creative direction established during pre-production. **b&a**

Page 12: These frames showcase Pixomondo's previs, the plate shoot and a live comp over the previs.

Page 15: A Pixomondo previs frame.

All images © 2024 HBO.

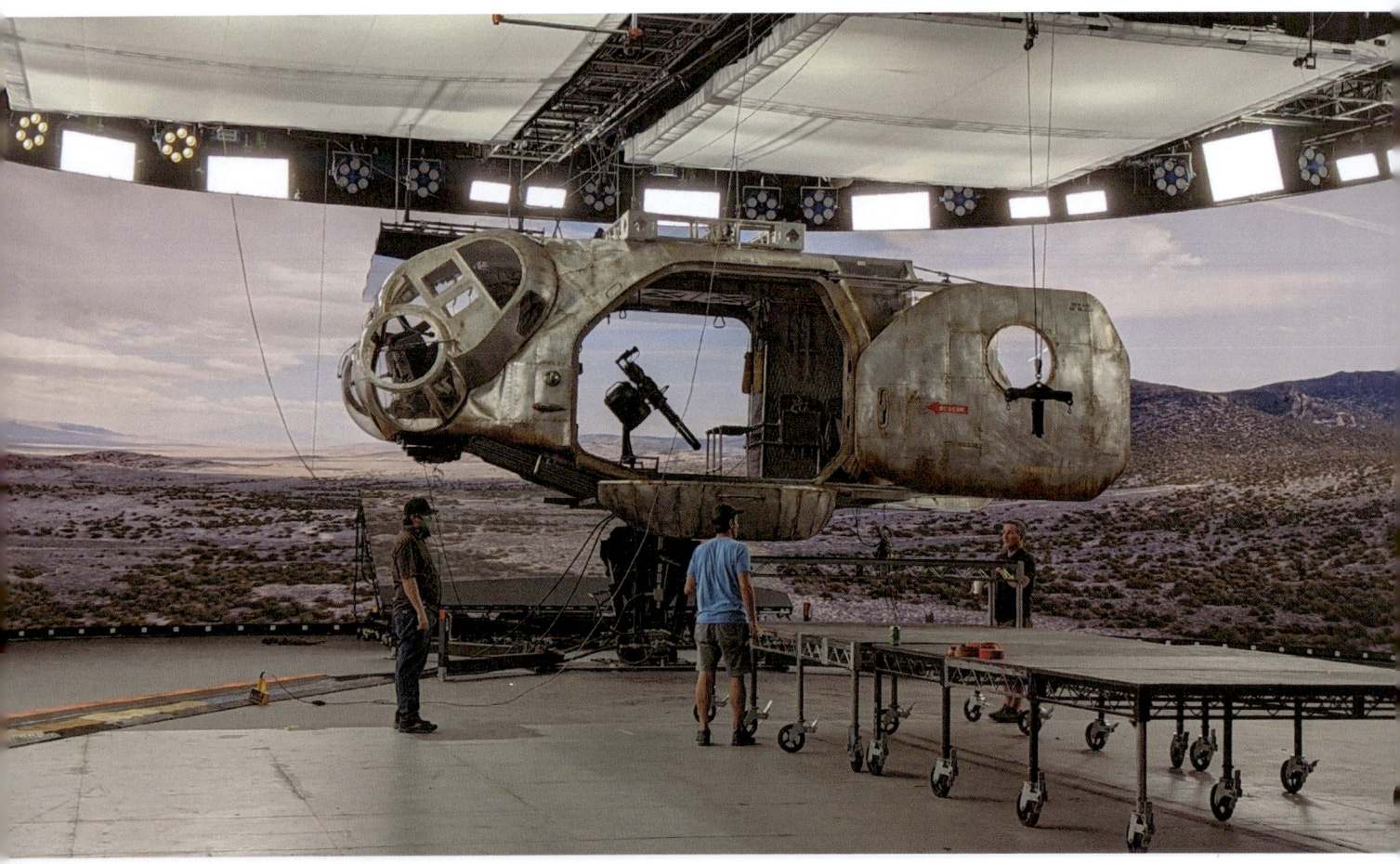

SHOOTING ON AN LED VOLUME...ON FILM

Magnopus details its particular virtual production approaches on Fallout, which included capturing the LED wall scenes on 35mm film. **By Ian Failes.**

The Prime Video post-apocalyptic series *Fallout* was shot on 35mm film with anamorphic lenses. While that's a format not unfamiliar at all to the show's executive producers Jonathan (Jonah) Nolan and Lisa Joy–who took the same approach on *Westworld*–it is a format not all that common for an episodic project that also relied heavily on shooting in an LED volume.

Getting there required close collaboration with Magnopus, a studio that had been part of previous *Westworld* R&D efforts and some filming (on film) in an LED volume for that series' fourth season. "That season four of *Westworld* was where the evolution of this tech, integrated into storytelling, really began," advises AJ Sciutto, director of virtual production at Magnopus.

Sciutto oversaw the effort at Magnopus to deliver and collaborate on several virtual production services for *Fallout*, including the virtual art department, LED volume operations and in-camera VFX (ICVFX). *Fallout's* visual effects supervisor was Jay Worth and visual effects producer was Andrea Knoll. The show's virtual production supervisors were Kathryn Brillhart and Kalan Ray, who oversaw four episodes of the series each. Magnopus ran stage operations for the first four episodes, with All of it Now handling the second lot of four episodes. More on how the film side of the production came into play below, but first the process began with the building of an LED volume in New York, where the series would be shooting.

"At the time," says Sciutto, "there was not an LED volume in New York that could have accommodated a show this size. Spearheaded by production's Margot Lulick along with our partners at Manhattan Beach Studios and Fuse Technical Group, Magnopus' CEO Ben Grossmann and the Magnopus team designed an LED volume in Long Island at Gold Coast Studios that was built to meet the specifications that Jonah wanted. He likes doing walk-and-talks, he likes being in longer shots, almost oners. He likes being able to be encompassed by immersive content. And so the design of the volume was very much a horseshoe shape. It wasn't cylindrical like you see in a lot of volumes now. It was a horseshoe to allow us a big long, flat section to do a walk and talk. The final LED wall size was 75' wide, 21' tall, and almost 100' long."

The assets for the LED wall–which included virtual sets for the underground vaults and post-apocalyptic Los Angeles environments–were designed to run fully real-time in 3D using Epic Games' Unreal Engine. "We used the latest and greatest versions of Unreal at the time," states Sciutto. "For the first couple episodes of the season, this was Unreal 4.27, and then we took a few months hiatus between the first four episodes and last four episodes and at that point Unreal upgraded to 5.1 and there were some advantages in using 5.1. Lumen was one of them, the real-time global illumination system, which we found to be pretty essential for the needs of the set designs that we were working with. And so we upgraded engine versions to Unreal 5.1 about a week before we actually shot the scenes using it, which can be a hive-inducing moment to anyone who's worked in this industry before. Epic says we were probably the first large production to actually use 5.1 in practice and it ended up working great for us."

MAKING IT WORK FOR FILM

With the LED wall stage established and virtual art department builds underway, Magnopus still needed to solve any issues arising from the shooting of 35mm film on the volume. Sciutto notes that genlock was the most important factor. "You have to be able to genlock the camera so that you're getting in sync with your refresh of the LEDs. We had worked with Keslow Camera back on *Westworld* to get sync boxes that are designed for the Arricam LT and Arricam ST to read a genlock signal and actually be able to phase lock the camera. That took a couple months of just designing the leading to trailing edge of the genlock signal for the camera to read that and get that to be in phase."

"Once we did a couple of camera tests," continues Sciutto, "we felt like we were in a good state, but then we had to do some wedge tests because the actual latency flow between Unreal to the render nodes to the Brompton processors to the screen was slightly dynamic. We had to do some wedge tests to figure out what that latency offset was so we could then dial in the camera."

The next hurdle was color workflow. "Normally," says Sciutto, "you build in a color profile for your camera, but because the HD tap on the film camera is not truly an HD tap, you are winging it. Well, you're not actually winging it. There's a lot of science behind it in terms of what you're looking at in dailies and how you're redialing the wall and how you're redialing to a digital camera. You can't really trust what you're seeing out of the HD tap. So we had a Sony Venice that was sitting on sticks right next to the film camera. We had a LUT applied to the digital camera that mimicked our film camera so that we could do some live color grading to the overall image of the wall."

Sciutto adds a further challenge was understanding the nature of different results from the film lab in terms of dailies. "Depending on which day of the week we got the dailies processed, they might change the chemical bath on Mondays, so by the end of the week it might skew a little bit more magenta or might skew more green. We would use the digital camera footage to know we were always within a very comfortable range."

That dailies process–which saw rushes shipped from New York to Burbank for development and digitization–also impacted the pre-light on the LED wall, as Sciutto explains. "When you do a pre-light day on the film camera, you don't really know what you shot until a day and a half after. So we would do a series of pre-light shoots where we would shoot on a day, get the film developed, have a day to review and make any adjustments to our content before we did another pre-light day. That created a schedule for us that allowed set dec to get in there and do some adjustments to the scene, or our virtual art department to do lighting adjustments to the virtual content to make sure it lined up with the physical content and be ready for any of the lighting and color settings we needed to be set up for on the actual shoot day."

Asked about the final look of the LED wall film footage, Sciutto mentions that "seeing the finished results in dailies, there was definitely a softer fall-off between your foreground actors, your mid-ground set pieces and your background virtual content. That transition was blended a little bit smoother through the grittiness of the film [compared to digital] and that helped a lot. Also, you can capture a lot more detail and range in film that allows for more dynamic offsetting through color in a post process than you can with digital. If you go digital and then you push it or you crank it

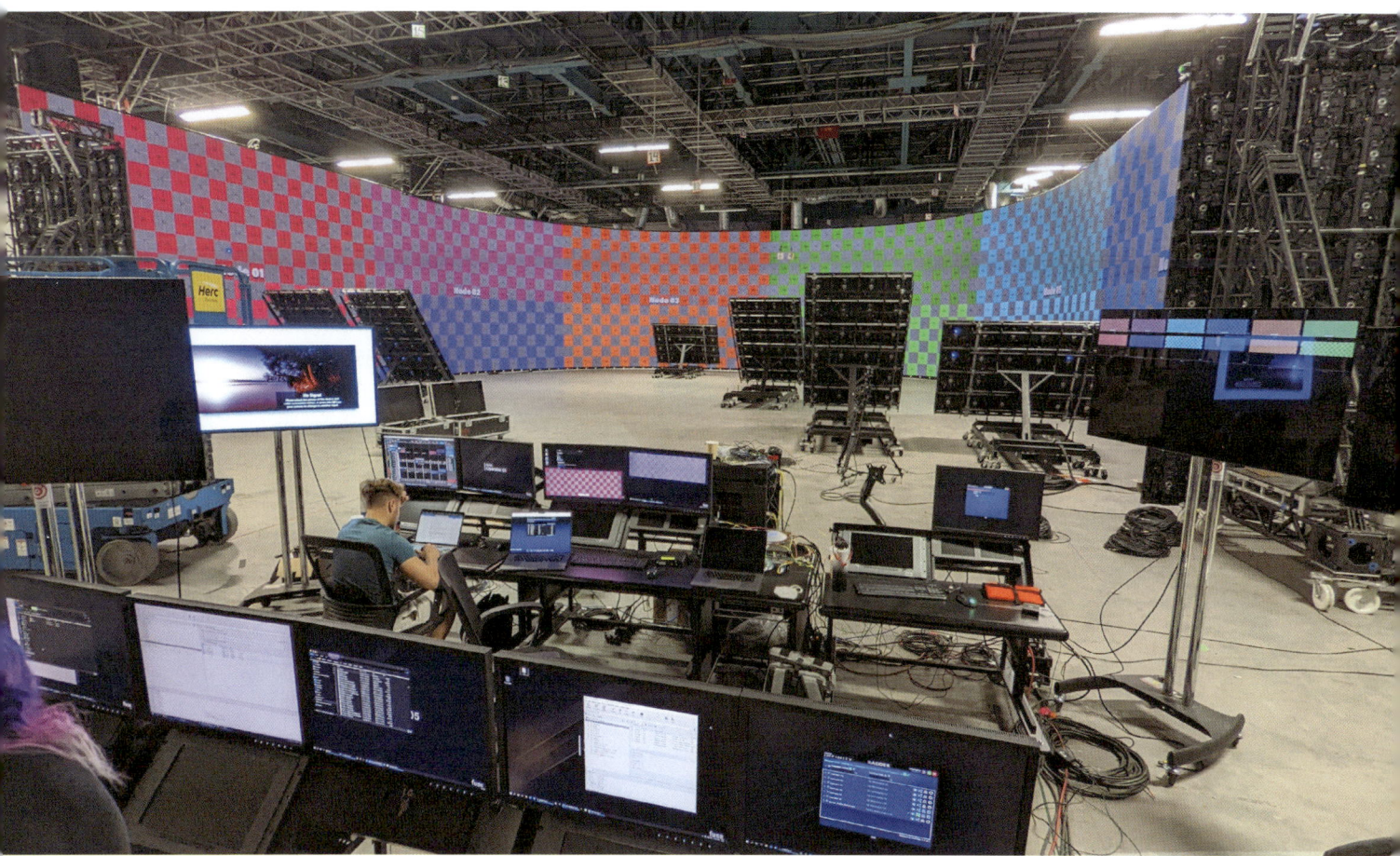

too much, it can get 'weird' somewhat quickly. So shooting on film at least allowed us more range to dial in during the DI."

DESIGNING FOR THE LED WALL

As mentioned, Magnopus ran the virtual art department (VAD) on *Fallout*. It was led by VAD supervisor Craig Barron, VAD lead Devon Mathis and lookdev/lighting supervisor Jeremy Vickery. Video game development company Virtuos also assisted on the builds. The VAD had 16 weeks to design, build, and optimize virtual sets to run on the LED wall. The largest virtual asset build was for the vault cornfield farm location, crafted by production designer Howard Cummings. A signature element in that set was the projector systems set up to 'project' painted farmland views on the vault walls for the vault dwellers. "We worked with Jonah and Howard to figure out how the projector systems would've worked in the 1950s to project light onto the screens and what kind of translucent backing the screens or the walls would've had," describes Sciutto.

The vault farm was designed as a room that was bigger than the LED volume itself, indeed, bigger than any LED volume in the world. "What that meant," says Sciutto, "was that on set we had a physical build that was a portion of a 3D virtual build which was extended by a 2D background build. The physical build included prop corn stalks, which we scanned, digitized, photogrammetized, and made CG corn as a middle ground layer, and then extended that into a matte painting. We brought on Rocco Gioffre and Frank Capezzuto III to art direct how we'd achieve the build out, and then create the incredible matte paintings that extended the cornfields and farmland from the practical corn. The blending of that transition was important. Obviously you're not going to get movement in the corn from wind detail in the matte painting, but the 3D corn had a bit of wind effect on it to blend that transition with the practical corn on set."

"We also had to keep in mind that Howard and the art department were building the reverse angle of the vault on a stage in Brooklyn," continues Sciutto. "So we sent our photo acquisition team and our LIDAR team lead by Fabian Flores and Devon Mathis out to that stage and hosed that down with photography for photogrammetry and LIDAR scans so that we could use that for photo projection. We built the cornfield in a way that was somewhat symmetrical, so when we wanted to turn around, all we had to do was rotate the LED world 180 degrees, move one or two set pieces and we were back to shooting after lunch. Then when shot back at the vault dwelling wall inside the volume, it matched the physical build that was 75 miles away because we did all the photo capture from that set build."

While the virtual sets were built in traditional ways with traditional tools such as Maya, 3ds Max and Blender, the important factor here was to optimize them for running on the LED wall in Unreal Engine. Once modeled, layout of the assets took place directly in the game engine. "Then once we got a gray box environment," details Sciutto, "our viz lead Kat Harris put Jonah and the DP into that environment, allowed them to do some VR scouting, some virtual blocking of where the actors were going to go, and then let them work out how they were going to shoot it and where they were going to put lights, set pieces, stunt rigging, etc."

About a month before shooting, the DP worked with Magnopus to add virtual lighting inside the set. Here they would add lights and dial in exposure and luminance to the virtual set. Then a fortnight before the shoot, the asset would be loaded into the volume and here the DP would carry out practical lighting. "There was a lot of back and forth between the practical lighting and the virtual lighting," states Sciutto, "making sure that if we swung a light or if we moved something that we had a matching version of that light in real-time and that we could make those adjustments on the fly. Many of the movie lights on stage were controlled through Unreal via a DMX integration created by Addison Herr, ensuring the lighting color and detail matched the virtual set."

In one particular moment involving the cornfield farm, things go awry during a wedding sequence. It results in the 'projectors' being shot and the projected screen showcasing a film burn effect. This was an effect displayed live during the shoot. "We had our Houdini guys Justin Dykhouse and Daniel Naulin working on that effect for a month or two," recalls Sciutto. "They looked at a lot of reference of burning celluloid, especially what that looked like in the 1950s. It was difficult not only just to build an effect that looked like burning celluloid, but we had to do that across a 16K canvas being rendered on 8 different render nodes. It couldn't just be a 4K video output. What we built allowed us to stop on a moment and go back into playback so that we could redo a take without having to go too far forward into the effect."

Another key moment sees lead character Lucy leave her vault to enter the wasteland. Here the design was based on the entrance from Vault 76, a vault from 'Fallout 76', one of the game installments on which the show *Fallout* is based. The only set piece there on the day of shooting was the elevator, the floor, the bridge and the vault door. Everything else was an Unreal Engine asset.

"That was probably one of our most successful asset loads," marvels Sciutto. "We shot that entire sequence in a day. That asset held up phenomenally. Because our volume was a horseshoe and the vault door was in the opening of the horseshoe, there was some missing coverage needed between where the volume ended and practical set began. Jay Worth and Andrea Knoll and their VFX teams did a fantastic job in doing some set extension to marry those two things together, but everything that was shot of the vault itself, including shooting back into where the cargo area was, that was all done in the volume."

"It was also a fun scene," adds Sciutto, "because when we walked on set during rehearsals, it was decided we wanted to do a dynamic lighting change. As Lucy exits the elevator and enters that space, we wanted the lights to turn on. We took that asset and designed, all in very quick time, a dynamic lighting shift for that opening shot. We brought the system down during lunch, loaded the new lighting setup, tested it and shot that shot right after lunch."

Later, for the Griffith Observatory scenes, Magnopus generated matte paintings built up as full 3D environments for the post-nuclear attack Los Angeles backgrounds. "We procedurally built the city of LA using open source map data and satellite data for street layout and building layout," outlines Sciutto. "We replaced geometry of that map data with apocalyptic building systems and asset packs that we built and developed so that the streets of LA actually matched to what you would actually see from the Griffith Observatory, and then we added dust layers and 200 years of debris build-up onto those streets. We designed the buildings with carve-outs for how the missiles would've hit them or how they would've been destroyed by the explosions."

"Then, once we all bought off on what that look was for the city, we built a few different lighting environments. We did one at pure dusk, we did one at sunset, we did one at nighttime with lights on for the city and lights off for the city, once the power gets turned back on. These were dynamic loads of the asset based on which lighting condition it was. All the work that went into building that 3D environment got rendered out as a 2D matte for the far background, allowing us to shoot that scene at extremely high efficiency and frame rate."

THE VOLUME AND VERTIBIRDS

A different kind of LED wall challenge came in the form of the Vertibird vehicle flying scenes. For these moments, characters were often seen taking off or during flight looking out onto the environment around them. Here, Magnopus handled the work as video playback on the LED wall, which surrounded a Vertibird set piece.

"For these scenes," breaks down Sciutto, "we knew they needed to be photoreal environments surrounding the Vertibird. Our viz lead Kalan Ray virtually plotted a helicopter path using accurate time of day studies and satellite data to allow us to see the exact terrain and environment we'd be shooting within. Jay Worth found a drone capture team that used a 180 degree 12K three camera capture array, which then got stitched and converted into playback video for us. The Vertibird set piece was on a mechanical base and was married to playback. What that allowed us to do was capture the scenes in-camera through video playback."

"The fun part about that was we had these wild walls on set," says Sciutto. "They were four by six LED panel tiltable walls that were on rollers and casters that we could slide around the stage. Our camera tracking team 3D printed camera tracking beacons for those walls. As we rolled them around the stage, the projection surface was changing as they were being projected on, based on where they were in the volume. Those were helpful in filling in the little gaps that we would see from the Vertibird setpiece being in the middle of the stage. For example, we'd be shooting down on the pilot, so we needed to fill in the floor. We'd just roll in the wild walls there, have that map the projection surface to it and we could just shoot with the same video content. It worked great." **b&a**

Page 16: A partial Vertibird set-piece in the LED wall volume is readied for filming for Fallout.

Page 19: The LED volume in Long Island at Gold Coast Studios.

Page 20: The LED wall was 75' wide, 21' tall, and almost 100' long, in a horseshoe shape.

Page 21: Behind the scenes of the corn farm wedding LED wall set.

Pages 22 & 23: The LED wall, and the scene as it appeared in the show.

Page 24: All the LED wall sets mixed practical set-pieces with LEDs.

Page 27: Lucy's vault exit sequence was a blend of real and virtual.

Page 28: Inside the Griffith Observatory LED wall set.

All images © 2024 Amazon Prime Video.

IN THE VOLUME WITH GLADIATORS, CHARIOTS AND HORSES

A round-table discussion on the virtual production challenges of Those About to Die. **By Ian Failes.**

Roland Emmerich's Peacock series, *Those About to Die*, tells the story of the Roman Empire's games. The show relied on virtual production techniques to bring audiences into key locations, such as the 80,000 seat Colosseum to witness dramatic chariot racing.

Production filmed at a revolving LED volume setup at Cinecitta Studios in Italy. Visual effects supervisor and second unit director Pete Travers and visual effects producer Tricia Mulgrew collaborated with Dimension Studio, DNEG and ReDefine to deliver VP and VFX services, ranging from Roman environments to crowds and even pre-rendered horses.

In this round-table with *befores & afters*, Travers is joined by virtual production supervisor James Franklin (Dimension Studio) and visual effects supervisor Izet Buco (ReDefine) to break down the VP aspects of the show.

b&a: Pete, how were you and Roland Emmerich planning to use virtual production on the show? Tell me about the early conversations you had about this with him.

Pete Travers (production visual effects supervisor and second unit director): Well, the first kinds of conversations–and these happened months before pre-production–were about determining where we shoot. We ended up visiting Cinecitta Studios, which is the famous studios in Rome. There were tremendous advantages to shooting at Cinecitta, in particular, because they had shot the HBO miniseries *Rome* back in the day. There was also the recent *Ben-Hur* movie and that came into play because they had put a chariot racetrack at Cinecitta World, which is a Universal Studios-like amusement park. What it meant was there was a backlot of the Forum and the track from *Ben-Hur*.

Then, the pièce de résistance was that they had actually built an LED stage there that had been barely used. And it was *big*. The joke we made was that it was a little bit like *Field of Dreams*: 'If you build it, we will come'. It was eight meters tall and had a total circumference of approximately 51 meters, in a U-shape. So, we got there and we were like, well, there's nothing else that comes close to this place.

Now, there was the LED wall, but there were no guts, so to speak, for the wall. Tricia Mulgrew, my visual effects producer, and I had to aggressively find a partner not just for visual effects but for virtual production and previs as well. DNEG and Dimension were unquestionably our best choice. With this being a television program and with the appetite of Roland Emmerich to do 10 hours of television at Roland Emmerich ambitions, we needed a partner that was very, very willing to work within the budget that we had. I had a number of great conversations with DNEG 360/Dimension

Studio managing director Steve Griffith. It was almost like we instantly had a shorthand, and that's how we got started.

b&a: What were some of the things you knew virtual production would be most useful for?

Pete Travers: Roland really wanted to do chariot racing on the LED wall. The idea was that we were going to film the charioteers riding on chariots with no horses in the foreground for the close-ups of the sequence, and then in the background we'd need horses. We had to figure out, how do we render the horses and how did we do crowds? The crowds, well, they have costumes. That means that the costume department had to complete the design of their costumes well before they usually have to do because we had to do a whole volumetric capture setup in London months before we started shooting. ReDefine would then have to render it all, including the stadium, and have it ready for the wall.

It really takes the entire typical schedule of film production, and completely reorders it. Typically in CG when you say, 'We need this quick,' that means a week or two. With virtual production, it means, 'We need it in an hour.' The only way to do that was to manufacture calendar time and there were some pretty harrowing moments. One thing James had to deal with right out of the gate was that we had to build another LED wall because we weren't ready on the main wall. It was because of actor availability with Anthony Hopkins. He was only available much earlier on, so we had to build a smaller wall for his scenes. It was like, 'Welcome to the show, you're behind already.'

James Franklin (virtual production supervisor, Dimension): [*laughs*] I think with hindsight, though, that was actually quite good because it was a good dry run for the big wall. I think if we'd gone straight into the big wall, it would've been daunting straight off the bat. So we were lucky that we first had a go at the smaller wall and got our feet wet. The smaller wall had a resolution of approximately 6K. It was a flat wall and we primarily used it for views outside of windows and off balconies. It provided a lot of lighting to the set itself. These sets are mainly made of marble and stone so you get a lot of bounce light. We were stopping down on the wall because the ISO was so high that the wall was just blowing out.

Pete Travers: That's an important point in that virtual production has a very important relationship with the camera and the camera that you pick. We were testing a lot of cameras, but the Sony VENICE 2 blew everything else out of the water when it came to its low light capabilities. We wanted the walls to do the work–the interactivity–with the shiny marble. When you typically do this kind of environment work in post you usually just throw up a bluescreen and you don't get any of that subtle bounce/interactive light that you would get on a VP stage. So, there's some things that would never look as good if we threw up a bluescreen and just did it as a comp in post.

b&a: Tell me more about chariot racing.

Pete Travers: Well, we knew early on that there was no way that we were going to get real-time horses. So we had to pre-render those. For Izet, that was his trial by fire I would say, and make that work for the big wall which was 16K. And then there was the crowd. On a typical VFX show, for designing something like the Circus Maximus, you have until about halfway in post to complete the design of any kind of major thing that you're doing, whether it's a creature or an environment. But here we had to have the design completed

in pre-production and then rendered while we were shooting other things. Luckily, we had some sense about ourselves that we pushed all the chariot racing stuff to the very end of the VP schedule.

Izet Buco (visual effects supervisor, ReDefine): To be honest, I never had a plan to do anything with virtual production. I'm a traditional visual effects supervisor. I went to Pete and Tricia's office and they said, 'Well, we need to do this in VP.' So we had to design all the creatures and all the Circus Maximus. We had to do crowd work with volumetric capture. All upfront. For the horses, we spent quite a bit of time scanning them. They of course needed to match the horses from the practical shoot. As Pete mentioned, we couldn't bring the horses into Unreal and start moving things around. It had to be pre-rendered and the challenge was it was 16K. Also, it had to be rendered as a cylindrical or lat-long because the whole wall was built as U-shape. And for the crowds, it all needed to be loopable so that it worked at any point in a take.

The problem becomes, if you try to make a loop and the clips don't match, that introduces all kinds of problems. The crowd had certain kinds of clothing and we designed particular tools for the clothing and the kinds of reaction to the chariots, where they might stand up and clap. It was quite tricky to nail but we managed to fill that whole stadium with real-time crowds.

James Franklin: For the crowds, we had 90 actors in London and out in Rome, and we captured 500 individual volumetric performances captured on the Polymotion Stage (a Dimension/MRMC partnership). For the actual Circus Maximus, which is live in Unreal, we had 32,000 animated characters. Normally in VFX, you have cards and you have the performance on the cards and you offset the timings so that the crowd agents all look different. Instead, because we shot volumetrically, we were able to extract the normal maps from the volumetric captures and apply those to the cards, which means we could relight the cards in real-time. So, they're self-shadowing, and if you change the time of day, they would look correct in terms of lighting–that was a new thing to us. We've done some tests since then and we've got that up to 80,000 characters, so we can fill a large stadium quite comfortably.

What we did in VP had to also match with what Izet's team was doing later in VFX, because when you see the wides and the aerials, the fans watching the racing were in different factions. So they were grouped in terms of colors but not religiously grouped because some people venture into different areas.

Pete Travers: I had the opportunity as second unit director to direct all of the chariot race stuff, the practical stuff around the track. And of course, from all the nightmares that I've worked on in the past where you don't have the vital reference that you need to do something in post, I'm like, okay, well, while I'm shooting the direct photography that is going to go into the show, I'm also shooting reference of horses charging in chariots because I knew that Izet was going to need that reference, too.

The dynamics of the riding turned out to be the toughest thing. It's always surprising because you're thinking, okay, all the horses are all going to be super coordinated. But then we get there and we're watching it, and it's chaos. Those horses are bumping into each other, some horses are biting other horses and dirt's flying everywhere. It's a mess, but it looks really good. All of that stuff for VP had to be synthesized and mimicked and it worked.

Izet Buco: It was always great to have the real reference to what you're matching to. We followed a traditional process for the VFX by building the horses, going from bones to groom. Then it was just about how fast we could build them and render in such high resolution. We knew upfront where the priority was so we could in the early stages start spreading teams across from environments to the creatures to effects.

James Franklin: That's a good point actually. On a wider note–and Pete and Tricia were very clear about this from the start–you are one team. There was a good chance that Izet was going to go and build environments that we were building in Unreal and vice versa. We also had a fantastic production designer, Johannes Muecke, who was designing interiors as well. But we don't want everyone building things twice in their little silos. We live in a digital age where we can quite easily share assets. So, you have to have that oversight to say, okay, if Johannes has built a fantastic interior, which he did on one of the scenes, can we use it? Why would we go off and rebuild it?

Pete Travers: Yes, and in terms of the chariot racing, which is the pre-rendered scene, the vast majority of the rest of the work involves Unreal and doing things with a Rome model. We acquired a Rome model from a company in Germany and quickly handed it off to DNEG/Dimension so that they could start using it. I would say there was a tremendous amount of modification to it. But nevertheless, it gave us a great head start. We had to figure out ways to manufacture calendar time and we knew if we didn't do something like this–if they were designing Rome from scratch–we wouldn't have made it. Then of course we also gave it to both Izet and James so that James could start getting these environments ready in Unreal on the wall.

There is another component of the VP thing and the rescheduling that's worth mentioning, and that is with plate shoots you typically do it at the end of production. But all of our plate shoots had to be done before we started shooting. Tuscany was our key landscape location for Ostia Harbor, which is Rome's main harbor, but the real Ostia is not what you want to shoot. You need to find some pristine area that you can add ancient Roman buildings to. So, the scheduling of the plate shoot and also the value of the plate photography was monumentally important because it helps you not just completely rely on Unreal but rely more and more on plate photography. In fact, there are some shots in the show that I don't think people will realize were shot indoors.

Johannes the production designer had built this beautiful tent for the scene in episode 10. I am looking at it going, 'That just totally looks like it's outside.' And that was actually a very important conversation Roland and I had at the very beginning, saying, let's try to rely on as much plate photography as we can and put it on the wall because if you shoot it right and you get it right, then it works great.

The trick with it, and this is the big part about VP and where the advantage of VP lies, is for magic hour, I think. Even that term is a lie because magic hour lasts for about 15 minutes. It's not an hour. But if you can shoot these plates and get these things, then you can walk into magic hour and magic hour becomes *magic day*; it can last all day long. That being said, we also heavily relied on HDRIs and Dimension/DNEG 360 built this awesome cloud mover tool. That was proprietary, right, James?

James Franklin: Yes, because we had these beautiful skies with amazing clouds in them and we didn't want them to be static. So we came up with a way of using flow maps and various other techniques to very gently animate the clouds in a believable way, but more importantly on a loop so that

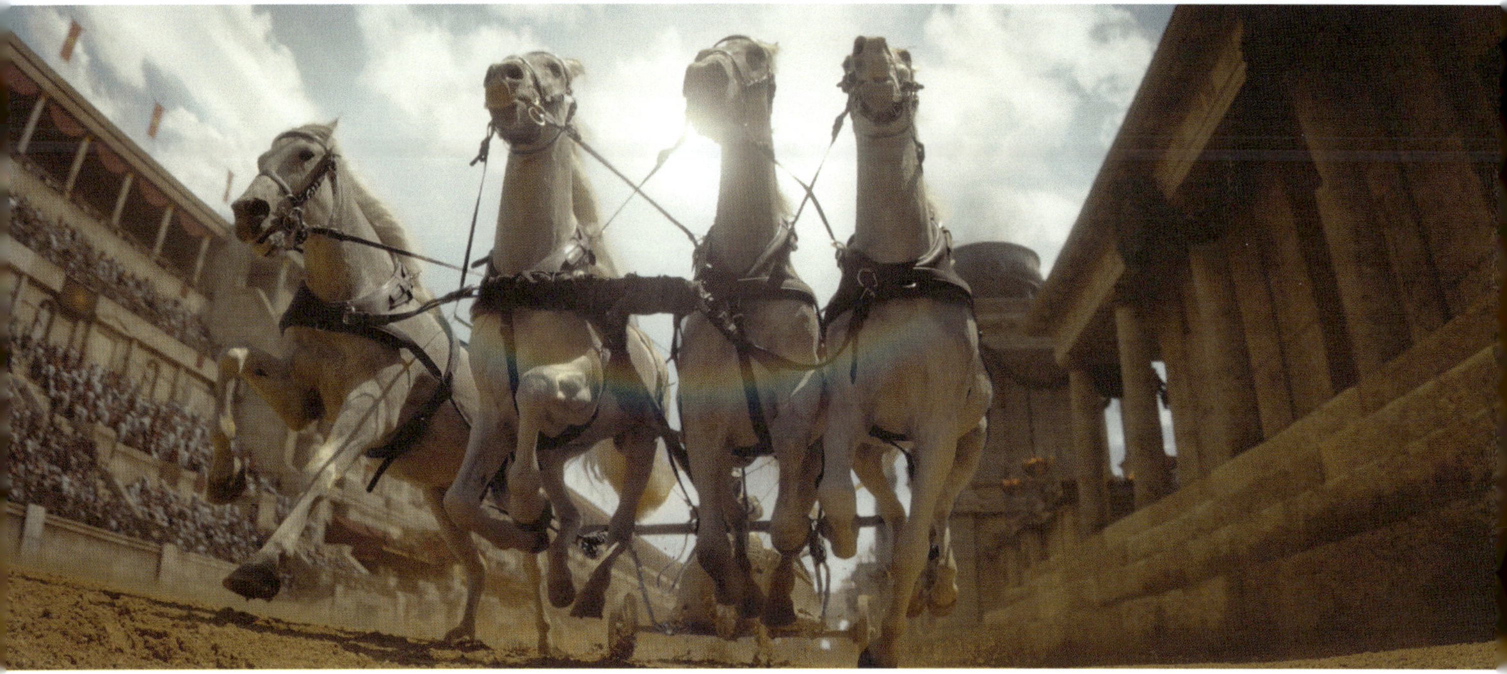

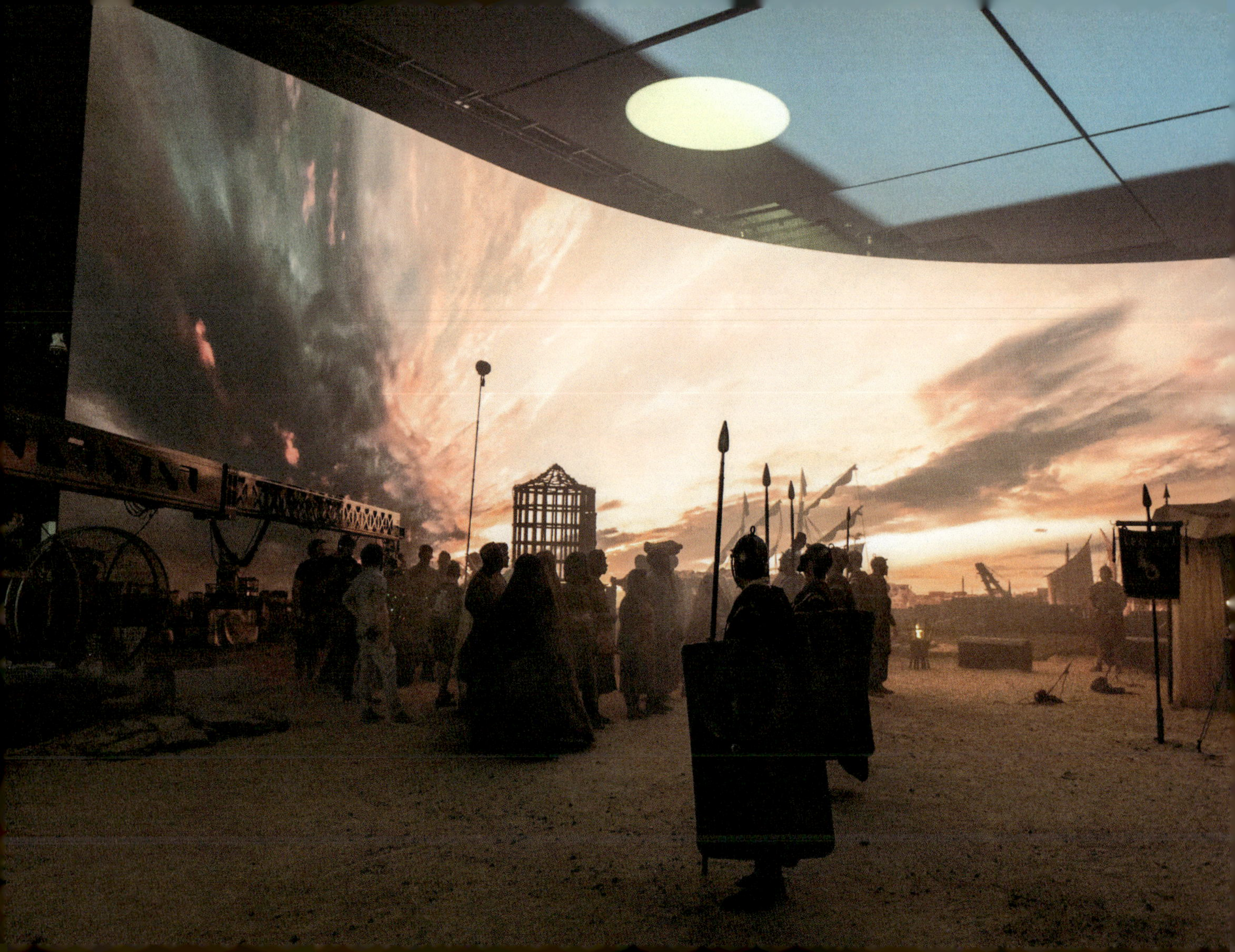

when we were shooting, we didn't have to go, 'Oh, sorry, you have to cut there because we've had a jump in the clouds.'

It was essentially a two-and-a-half-D scene. We had these HDRIs that were being animated in Unreal. We had some 360 degree photographic captures that Pete's team had gone out and captured for us that were placed in front of the sky. In the mid-ground, we added 3D geometry and things like the sea as well to give it parallax, and then Johannes' set dressing in front. So you had all these layers so it didn't just look like a flat plate.

b&a: I have a question about the nature of 'in-camera' visual effects or what is sometimes called 'final pixel'. In so many productions I've covered in recent times, there's such a mix of attempting to go for something in-camera or final pixel with no visual effects effort afterwards. Sometimes that's absolutely not the intention. The LED wall shoot is, instead, for great lighting reference and immersion of the crew and actors. What ended up being the approach with Those About to Die?

Pete Travers: Well, that comes down to Roland. The only way the VP is going to work is if you have a director that embraces the technology or if you have a director that says, 'I want this and I don't care how we get it, just make it happen.' There's a lot of stories about people throwing out VP, but Roland is not one of those guys. At a certain point you can tell him we can't do that, but we can do this, and then he makes it work. All told, by the end of the show, we only had 800 shots to do in post, and we accomplished 1800 shots in-camera on the VP stage. That's at least a two to one ratio.

There were fixes that we would do, but they were intentional fixes. Most of the shots that were the intentional fixes were where we had shot sand on the floor and we had to blend the sand from the stage to our digital sand. It just made it so much easier sometimes to do that in post. We still have a lot of shots of sand meeting digital sand that we accomplished on the VP stage, but those were the ones where we would just get to a point where we're like, okay, we're going to spend too much time putting the color correction boxes in Unreal. So, at a certain point, we said, let's just shoot because we'll fix this in post. That's a quick fix. Less than 10 shots required that.

b&a: James, I read that the stage in Italy was a revolving stage. How did that help or impact the approach to running the stage or how did you take advantage of it?

James Franklin: The obvious answer is that you can do your reverses really, really quickly. You can say, we're going to shoot this way and then we'll redress and we'll shoot the other way. It took about less than a minute to rotate the stage and obviously we can rotate the content on the wall very quickly. You can just shoot in any direction very, very quickly.

Pete Travers: And we did. The rotisserie was flushed to the wall. Basically it's a giant lazy Susan that's 24 meters in diameter. We had horses on the set. We had giraffes on the stage. So we took advantage of building one set rather than shuffling the set around and redressing—we just rotated the whole damn thing. It was maybe five minutes to do a 360. And it was strong enough that we could put some pretty elaborate sets on there. I think in the end, because of that, there's a lot of scenes in the show that people are not going to realize were shot on a VP stage.

In particular, I would say the Ludus stage where all the gladiators would train–the lighting was great there. The integration James's team built was fantastic. The only thing there on set was some sand and a little piece of fence. The immediate stands and then the building around was all in Unreal and the detail on it was magnificent. We even had digital characters walking back and forth.

b&a: Also, James, you used Unreal Engine but I think you also used TouchDesigner. How was that employed here?

James Franklin: That was for plate playback. Initially we were playing out, as Pete mentioned before, 16K plates. And then on the smaller stage it was 6K plates. So you need a system like TouchDesigner that can handle that and will just run all day and keep playing those plates. You can build up plates in layers as well, a bit like in Photoshop where you can add various layers and it can handle various layers that are animated as well. So it was very, very reliable for us and quite simple to use as well.

Then we moved away from TouchDesigner when we got to the biggest stage. We wanted to use Unreal primarily because all our operators are Unreal operators and we only had a handful of TouchDesigner operators. It's also just simpler to be in one package. Unreal got an update part-way through shooting and it let us play 16-bit EXRs in real-time. Once we had that, it was like, okay, we'll do it in Unreal. Both of them tracked as well, so you have camera tracking in both so that it was not just a flat plate, and when you move the camera from side to side, it will react correctly.

b&a: What was the virtual production shoot like for the team?

Pete Travers: I would say it can be extremely high stress. I look at it as like we're doing some kind of Broadway play or stage play, and the stage play completely changes every three days. So there's a lot of scrambling. I think the world of visual effects is a little bit more typically like an office job and then the film production and those groups have to merge together. Honestly, that's why DNEG/Dimension was so important because they were ready to play ball with all of this stuff.

I can also get into the problems that we were having. There's all kinds of internet issues that we were having at Cinecitta and how DNEG/Dimension had to bring their whole creative crew building these backgrounds to Rome in order to get this stuff done. Everything was changing on the fly. We're switching things around because you're at the whim of what production is shooting. And, getting back to Anthony Hopkins and his availability, we had to hurry up and shoot him.

That actually saved the show's ass because Anthony Hopkins was our only SAG actor. Because he had a scheduling conflict, we shot him out early, and because we did that when the strikes happened in LA, we didn't skip a beat, we didn't lose a day and we shot through the entire summer and we were one of the few shows out there that was still going. That was a little bit of luck there, I have to say.

b&a: Pete, you mentioned learning on the way, but I'm curious if you wanted to share any major lessons learned that you would take forward if you did this all again. Anything you'd do differently next time?

Pete Travers: Well, I think we were in the ballpark. I wouldn't do any radical changes, but I think a big part of it is

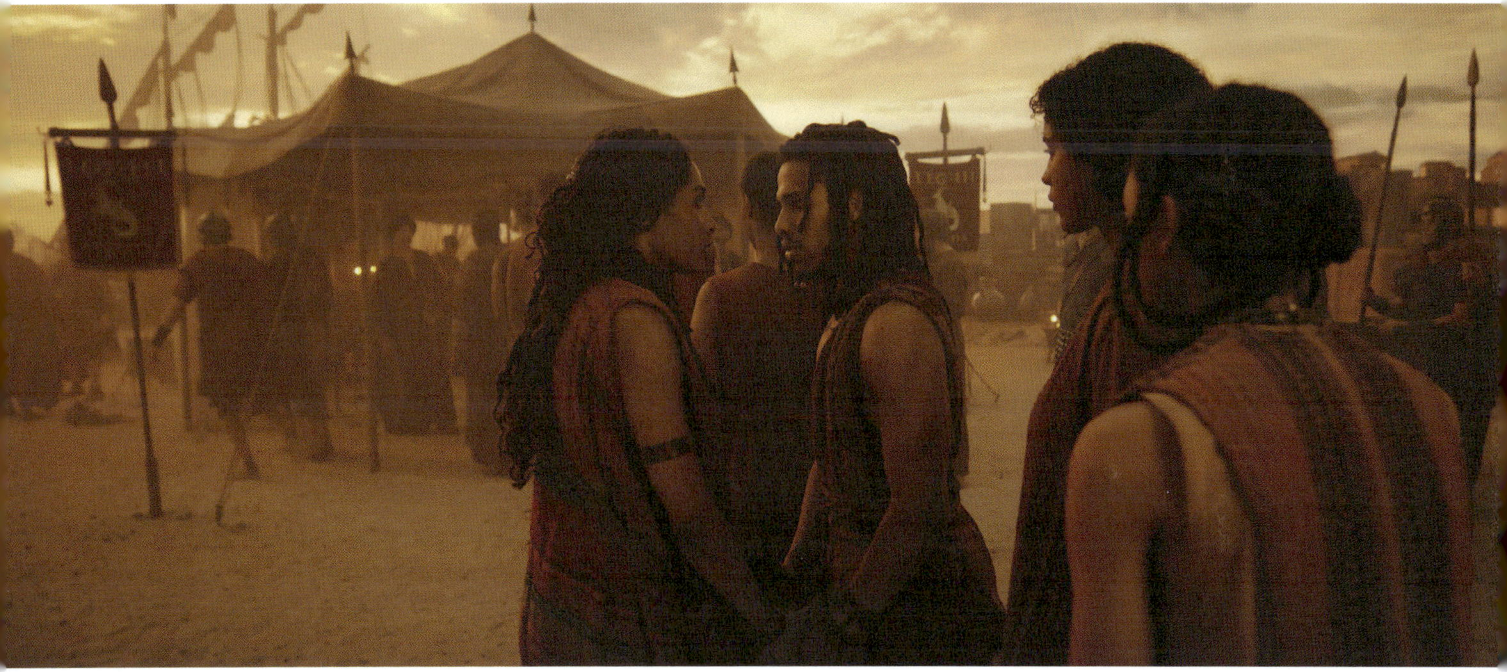

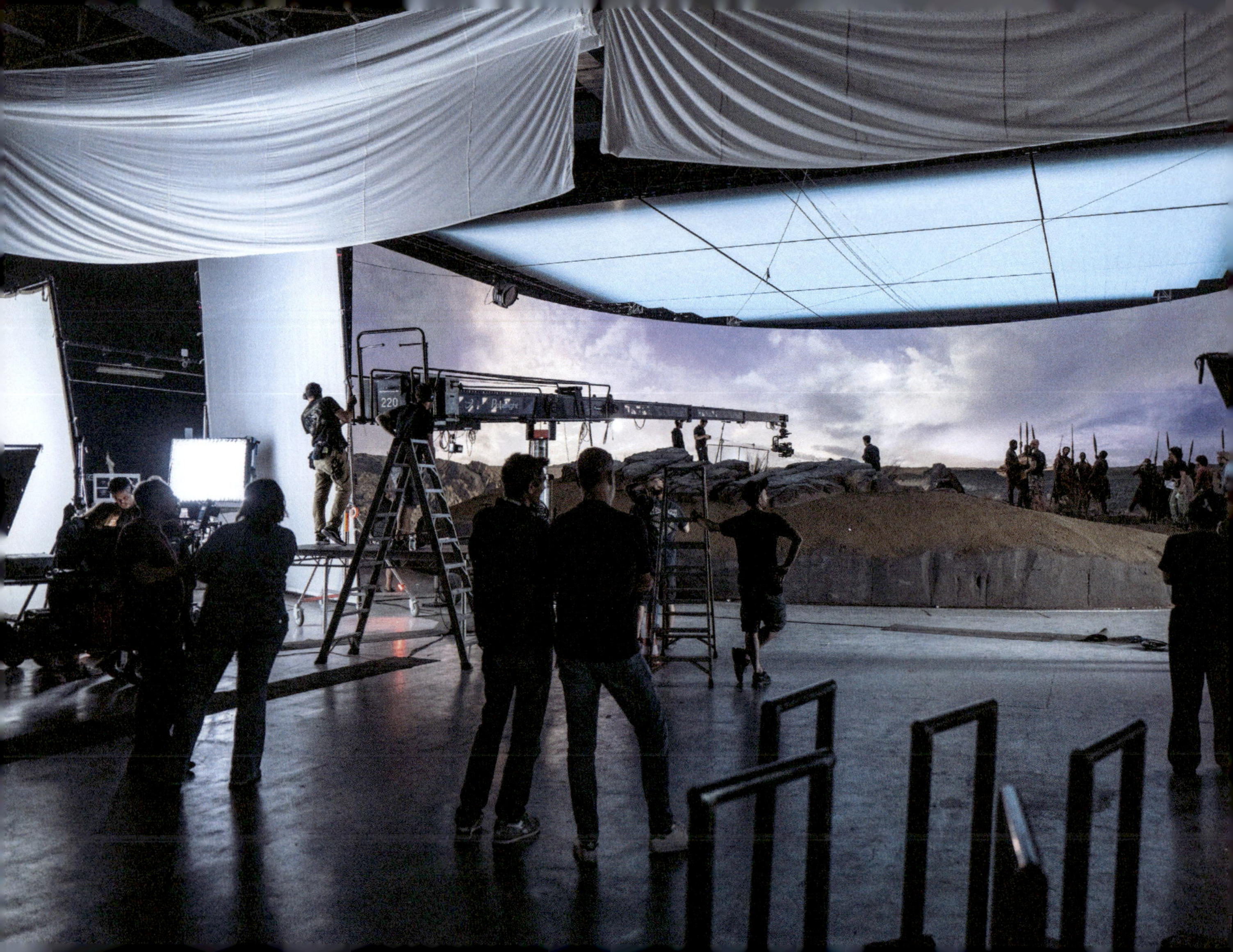

how the production would react to us. Typically, visual effects is like an afterthought. Typically, it's a couple of nerds running on set, throwing up a bluescreen and everybody's like, 'Who are these guys?' But for this show, by the end, everybody was on 'Team Wall'. So I wouldn't change anything.

It's not for everyone, it's not a complete solution. But then once you understand its use, and if it works for your show, you can make it work. VP was very much a technology that could be used on a show like this. I think for episodic television, and I certainly think for period television where you have a lot of backgrounds that you can't just go shoot—this is where VP is going to have its home. Sci-fi episodic, VP's also perfect for that.

James Franklin: Why Roland was great on this show was because you could say to him, 'Here's what normally happens on VP stages. These are the general rules.' Which, is a crazy thing to say. It's so new there aren't really any rules! Roland would take that on board, then he would do his own thing anyway, which would often make us look like absolute chumps because we told him it wouldn't. And so he, in his own way, pushed forward what we thought couldn't be done on the VP wall. Wide angle lenses, for example. You can't use wide angle lenses because you just get moiré everywhere. But Roland found out a way to make it work.

Pete Travers: Roland lived on an 18mm. He was living on an 18mm and he was far away. He's off the stage on an 18mm and it's like, 'Oh God'. Everybody's squirming. But we figured it out. Roland went to where it broke and then went just back inside to where it didn't break. Luckily the show was 2.35:1 because if it was 1.77:1 (HD), we wouldn't have been able to get any of our shots. The top of 2.35:1 was right there at the top of the wall.

Izet Buco: Actually, that's quite interesting, because we were looking at previs at any early stage and it was initially all 35mm and 40mm stuff. I had that in my mind when I was designing the VFX that it was all going to be really out of focus. But eventually all the shots were filmed where everything was opened up, and it did look really great.

Pete Travers: I think people would be shocked to find out the size of that stage for some of these environments that we did, like the workers' encampment with the sea of tents in front of the Colosseum. People would be shocked at how relatively small the VP stage that we shot at was and how much we made it look much bigger than it actually was.

James Franklin: We did away with the inner frustum in the end because there was just no point having one. We were shooting more of the stage with the wall than we weren't. So the whole point of a frustum is you're shooting selected areas, but if you're shooting that whole wall, you may as well not have it.

Pete Travers: Roland's the General Patton of filmmaking, it is a kind of Blitzkrieg approach. But in the end, he is blowing past all these barriers that we perceive but he ended up getting it done. **b&a**

Page 30: Roland Emmerich and Dimitri Leonidas, who plays Scorpus, discuss a chariot scene from Those About to Die inside the LED volume.

Page 33: A final shot of Scorpus from the series.

Page 34: The LED volume set up at Cinecitta Studios was eight meters tall and had a total circumference of approximately 51 meters, in a U-shape.

Page 37: A final chariot race shot.

Page 38: Dimension/DNEG 360 produced a cloud mover tool that could simulate cloud movement on the LED wall.

Page 41: A final shot from the series for an encampment scene that utilized the LED wall.

Page 42: 1800 in-camera shots were accomplished on the LED stage.

Page 45: The LED stage was also a revolving one, essentially a 'lazy Susan' 24 meters in diameter.

All images © 2024 Peacock TV LLC. All Rights Reserved.

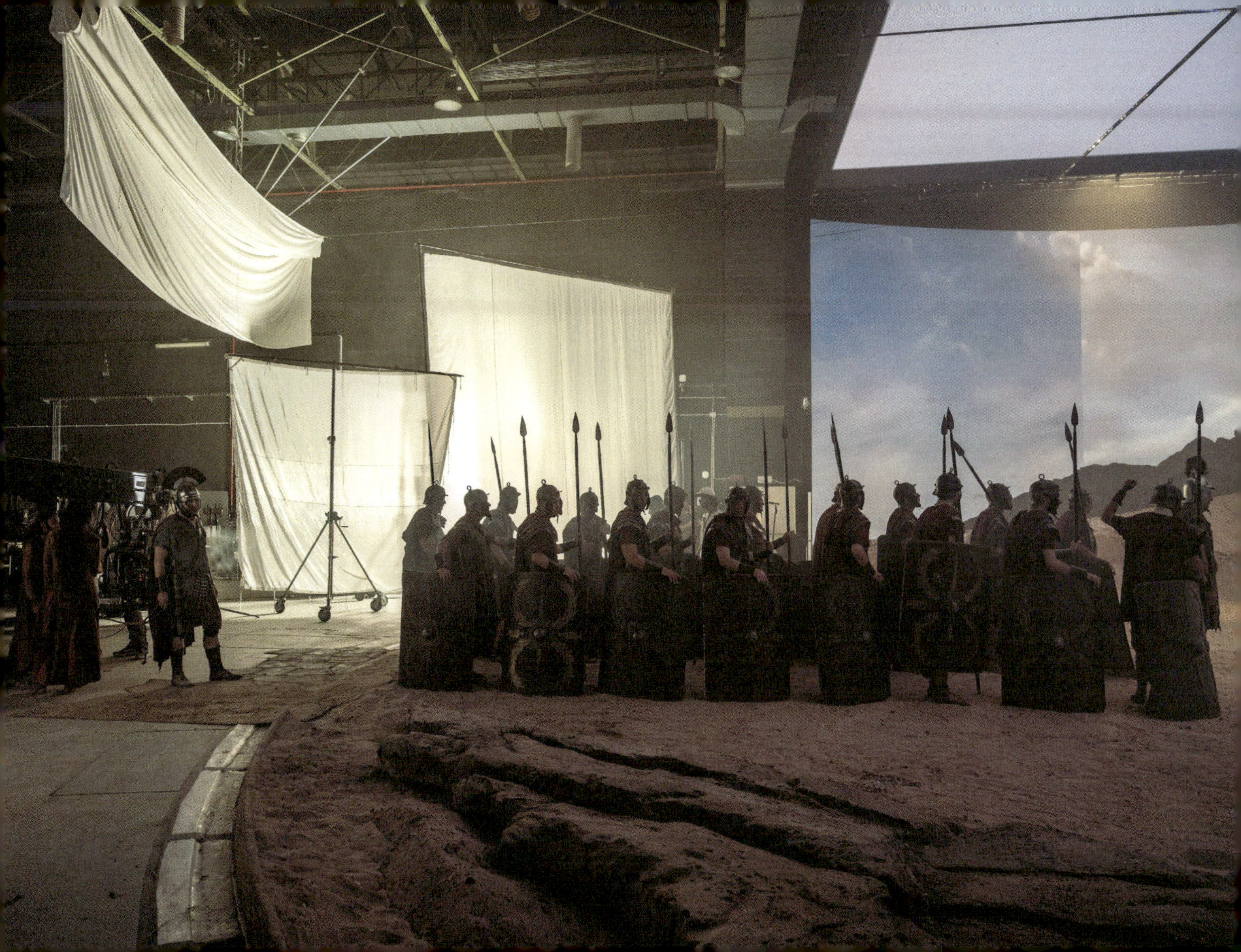

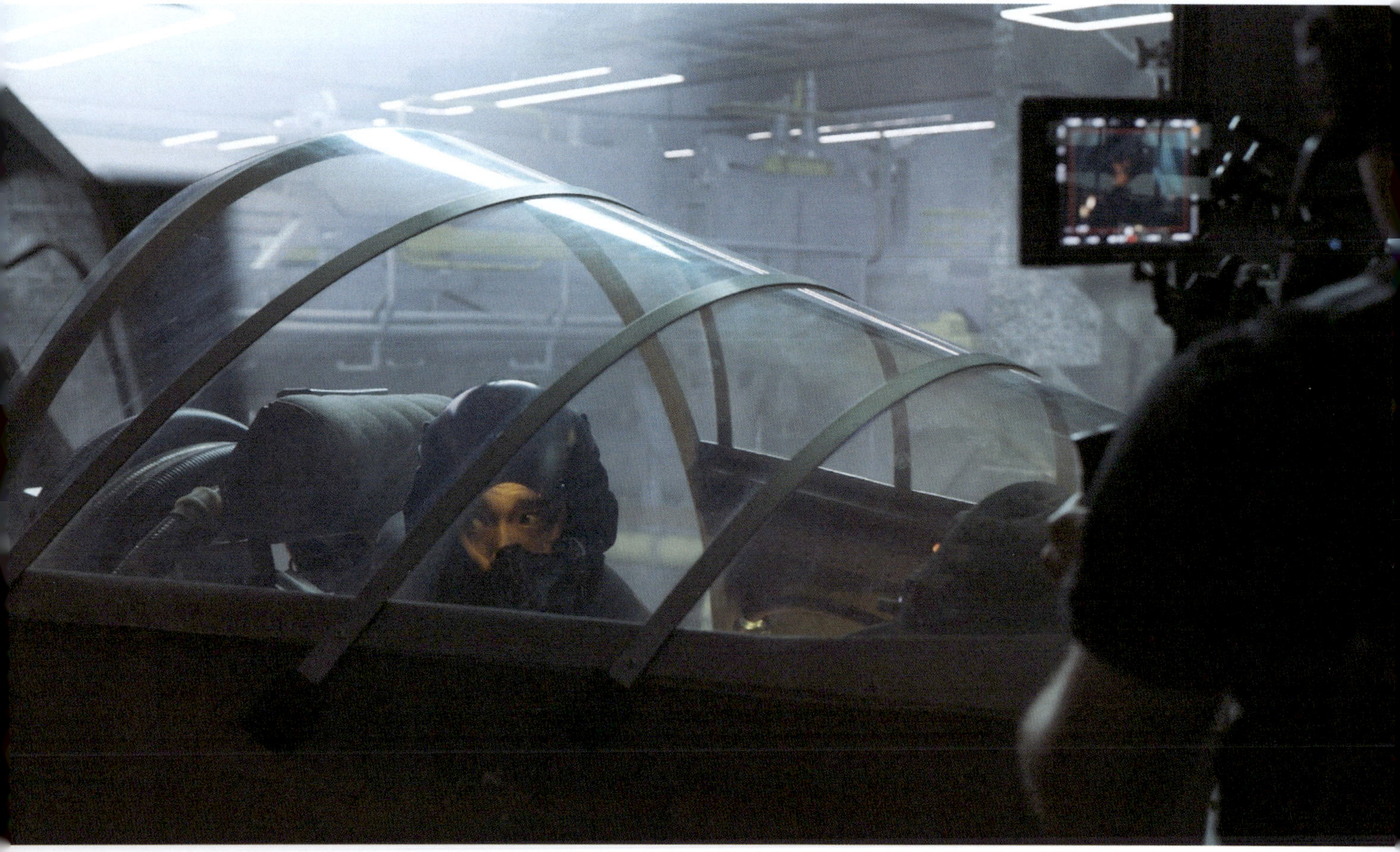

GETTING UP TO SPEED WITH LED WALLS FOR INDIES

How Impossible Objects is looking to make virtual production more accessible. **By Ian Failes.**

It's safe to say that many of the LED wall projects you hear about tend to be on large productions, including the ones covered in this issue of the magazine. But what about LED walls designed for smaller productions, indie projects or commercials?

One studio offering services exactly for those kinds of projects is Impossible Objects via its Culver City, CA facility. Having previously consulted on shoots involving larger volume stages, the studio has now installed its own. Director and founder Joe Sill touts the setup as a "more accessible volume stage solution that is a more nimble version of the ICVFX product, but is accessible to smaller budgets and productions, and to filmmakers who have yet to use or experiment with the tool because of the associated costs."

Impossible Objects' LED wall in Culver City is 30' wide and 10' high. It is built with AOTO 2.3mm pixel pitch panels, Brompton SX40 Tessera processors, and features a five-degree curve. It may be smaller than the world's largest virtual production volumes, but that does not mean the tech behind it is minuscule, as Sill outlines. "Key features of the stage include state-of-the art-render nodes, provided by Catalyst Virtual, and operator carts, featuring NVIDIA A6000 ADA GPUs, as well as a Mobile Cine' cart, where directors and cinematographers are encouraged to participate in modifying the virtual worlds seen on screen."

Music videos and car commercials are some of the projects that have been filmed on this LED wall stage. "Since our volume is new," admits Sill, "we have mostly been doing R&D for our larger entertainment projects, we used the wall as a visualization tool for a television show we're working on, and also created sales material for one of our original IPs. We've also done production for a narrative short film, several commercial automotive demos for car clients and are slated to do a few television commercials–our bread and butter–in the coming months."

Sill believes that all kinds of indie or smaller projects can benefit from LED wall shooting. "Our approach tends to be more affordable for indies overall because we're smaller with a lower overhead. It's easier for lower budget commercial or music video projects to shoot here, or for filmmakers who want to R&D virtual production before justifying the huge expense of getting up and running on a major volume."

Aside from the perceived cost, Sill says that the reason agencies and production companies might not necessarily turn their mind to virtual production is lack of knowledge about what it can bring to a particular shoot. "They need to know that it is an especially useful tool for inaccessible locations, imaginary locations, and/or an ambitious production that combines these two. They also need to understand that the tools live and die based on a great virtual art department that cleverly utilizes photoreal elements that make the virtual environments more believable."

"Game engine environments inherently limit the ability to photograph the fine details," details Sill, "but knowing how to navigate around those limitations is about both consulting with the DP ahead of time, giving them the ability to work with the art department to light environments and light and set dress the physical set to blend the two together.

"There is also more time spent in honoring the virtual art department process, there's more time spent upfront so when you're in production you're capturing visual effects where you don't have to do anything in post. If you prepare shots properly upfront, you don't need cosmetic readjusting or rotoscoping after the fact."

Impossible Objects itself began as a community of filmmakers and artists working in the area of virtual environments, virtual art department and creative needs of virtual production projects.

"We came to the realization that we needed to have access to the tools in our own backyard," shares Still. "So we built our own LED volume to continue to iterate and understand how to use ICVFX more effectively, and as a result we are able to R&D more frequently."

"The virtual production infrastructure supporting the LED wall, including direct connection to Impossible Objects' VAD team and environment library," adds Sill, "has been assembled to provide a streamlined process for filmmakers and is meant to help bridge the gap between traditional 'Brain Bars' and live action crew who might never interact with the virtual side of a production."

Which hopefully means more virtual production access, for projects large and small. **b&a**

Page 46: Behind the scenes of an LED wall shoot at Impossible Objects for their original IP project Cloud Racer.

Page 49: Impossible Objects' LED wall in Culver City is 30' wide and 10' high.

All images courtesy Impossible Objects.

48

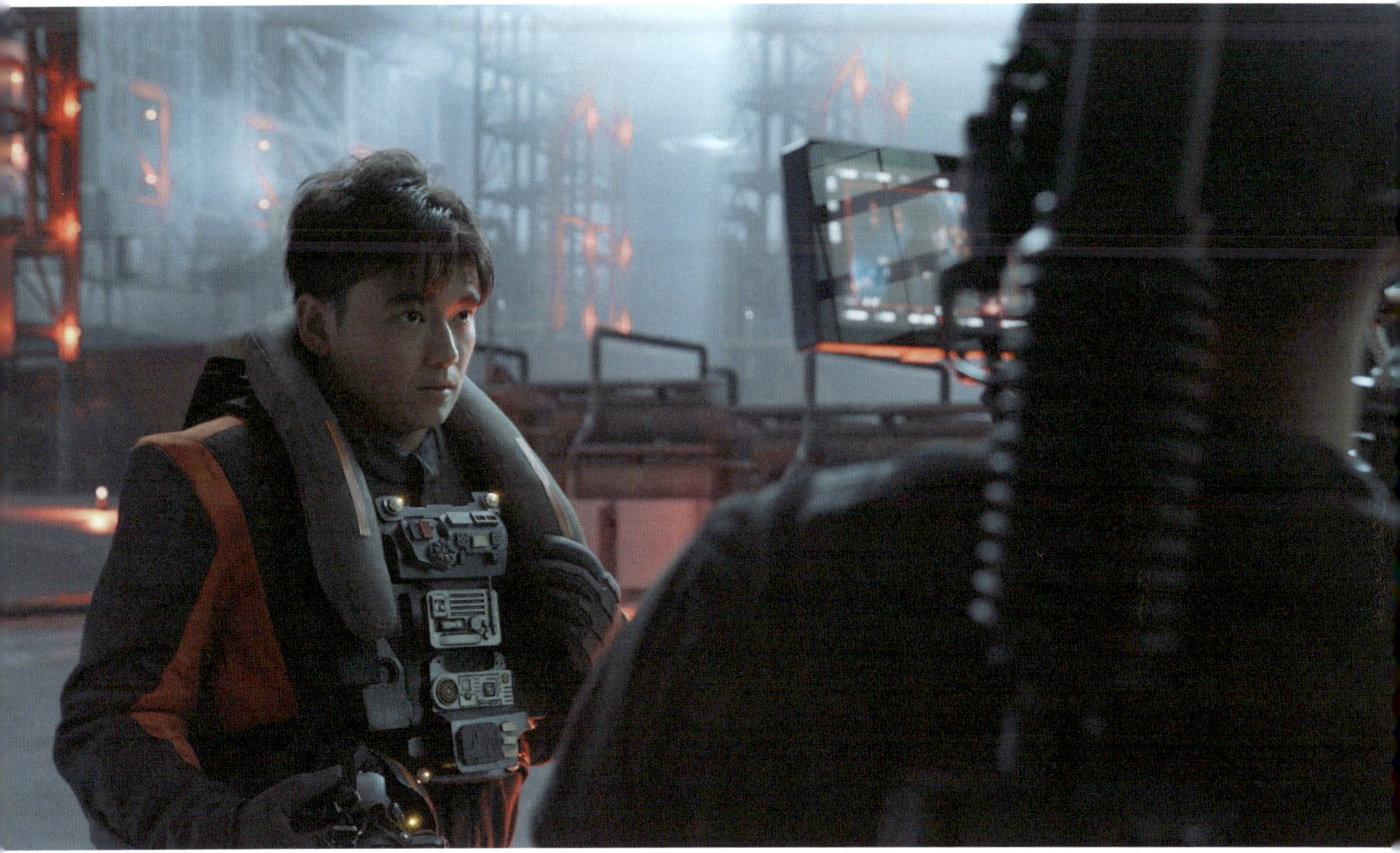

50

THE VIRTUAL TECH OF 'TED'

A look at the building of the ProVis tools on the first season of the Seth MacFarlane TV series. **By Ian Failes.**

When Seth MacFarlane's *Ted* television series was launched on Peacock earlier this year, *befores & afters* spoke to two members of the team behind the visual effects work. They were visual effects supervisor Blair Clark, a veteran of the *Ted* feature films, and Fuzzy Door Tech chief product officer Brandon Fayette. Fuzzy Door Tech is the technology division of MacFarlane's production company Fuzzy Door. On *Ted*, real-time tech in the form of ViewScreen was used to allow live-action actors to interact with a digital character during filming.

The tech–which has been dubbed 'ProVis'–allowed production to visualize the Ted CG asset in real-time on the set, and incorporated an iPhone-driven live capture of MacFarlane's performance, some pre-animation, and custom real-time animation via joystick during filming, too. Later, visual effects studios Framestore and Tippett Studio were responsible for crafting the final Ted performances.

Since this podcast was released, Fuzzy Door Tech has launched a number of related products: ViewScreen Studio, ViewScreen Scout Pro and ViewScreen Scout. I thought it would be interesting to go back to the original interview and hear how this virtual production tech was used on the *Ted* show. This is a cut-down version of the original chat.

b&a: What is this ViewScreen technology that you've pioneered for Ted and possibly other TV shows as well?

Brandon Fayette: It's a tool that allows us to take anything and put it directly in the camera's viewfinder. So, characters, set extensions, vehicles, spaceships, you name it, we put it in. It all started out on the third season of *The Orville* as a tool we were using to help make shot production go faster, landing shuttles and doing set extensions, and so on. And at that point it was more of a live performance tool, it didn't really have any ability to record or do anything like that. And it was used to doing 40-foot spaceships, giant creatures, not a small character like Ted. And when *Ted* came around, Seth and Blair were really receptive to us being able to use it on the show to enhance technology to record and to be able to do something with Ted.

We needed something we could use from location scouting to figure out how we were going to shoot the shot, to something we could actually film with. And we coined a term called production visualization or 'ProVis'. So you have previs and post-vis, we're doing pro-vis, shooting it live, and that's what we took to *Ted* to start bringing the character to life.

Blair Clark: My introduction to it was Brandon showing it to me, and what he had planned and constructed was ingenious. It would pipe a real-time representation of Ted into the viewfinders of the camera operators, so they could compose and track Ted, which normally would just be an empty plate. We had three cameras going on this show on any given shot. So out of those three, you'd always have one guy who's making assumptions that are a little different. So, this put them all focusing on the same target as if there was another actor right there, so it was extremely helpful that way.

b&a: It combines many things, doesn't it? In terms of live comp, live mo-cap to some degree, AR.

Brandon Fayette: Yes, I think there's always a challenge when you're trying to tell what we call the story of the shot, figuring out what we're trying to get across. I think there is a lot of back and forth that tends to happen between departments because they will see, say, the creature's head and not know that we're too close to the edge of frame. And so, now we have to digitally rebuild the top of a plate. Sometimes we can do a lot with mock-ups and stuffies, and things like that, but in certain scenes, in certain instances having that there is a lot less babysitting on the visual effects team, because the camera operators can adjust as needed. The fact that we're all having the same dialogue visually is great.

On *Orville* we used it for where we had people standing in front of a digital set extension of a shuttle or an environment. We would give the ADs iPads and they would hold it up and they would actually see, 'Oh, background is walking through the spaceship'. Instead of me putting tape on the ground or ping pong balls, they could self-fix it so there wasn't as much babysitting. And I think that's the big key as this technology in the industry evolves.

Blair Clark: As far as the operators and everybody on set, having something like this going on, even though we did use stuffies on this for lighting representation and a little bit of performance, if Ted's got to jump off the couch and exit the shot, there's somebody holding the stuffy who's got to get around the couch, get it out of the way, and so you've got this huge body and then a little bitty representation of Ted. So this just makes it very clear, it's clean, and it's just extremely helpful.

b&a: What were some of the technical hurdles you had to get over to implement this ProVis system?

Brandon Fayette: Getting the camera department on board is always a difficult thing with new technology. We had an advantage because the camera team that did *Ted* was the same camera team that did *The Orville*, so they were already familiar with this technology from a nascent level. So, it was figuring out how to mount it, figuring out how to synchronize and calibrate lenses, and so on.

And then of course there's also versions where there's moments in certain instances where Seth and Blair and team don't need to see Ted, they know where Ted needs to be, they just need a clean video feed. So, the camera operators would have their own feed versus what's happening in video village or what's happening on set, and being able to toggle between each side seamlessly so that people can get the information that they need in the moment is always something that's a challenge as well, I think. So we've built a lot of workflows and pathways to get people to do that.

Then obviously there's the latency. On *Orville*, we were about eight frames of latency and now we're four frames, so we're operating as fast as human muscles can expand and contract for the most part, at least optically.

b&a: I remember on the first film at least, and possibly on the second one, that Seth would wear an Xsens suit to do some live motion capture. I mean, it always made for great B-roll, but I imagine there were some challenges with that, Blair, of just getting that to work for TV? What was done differently this time around?

53

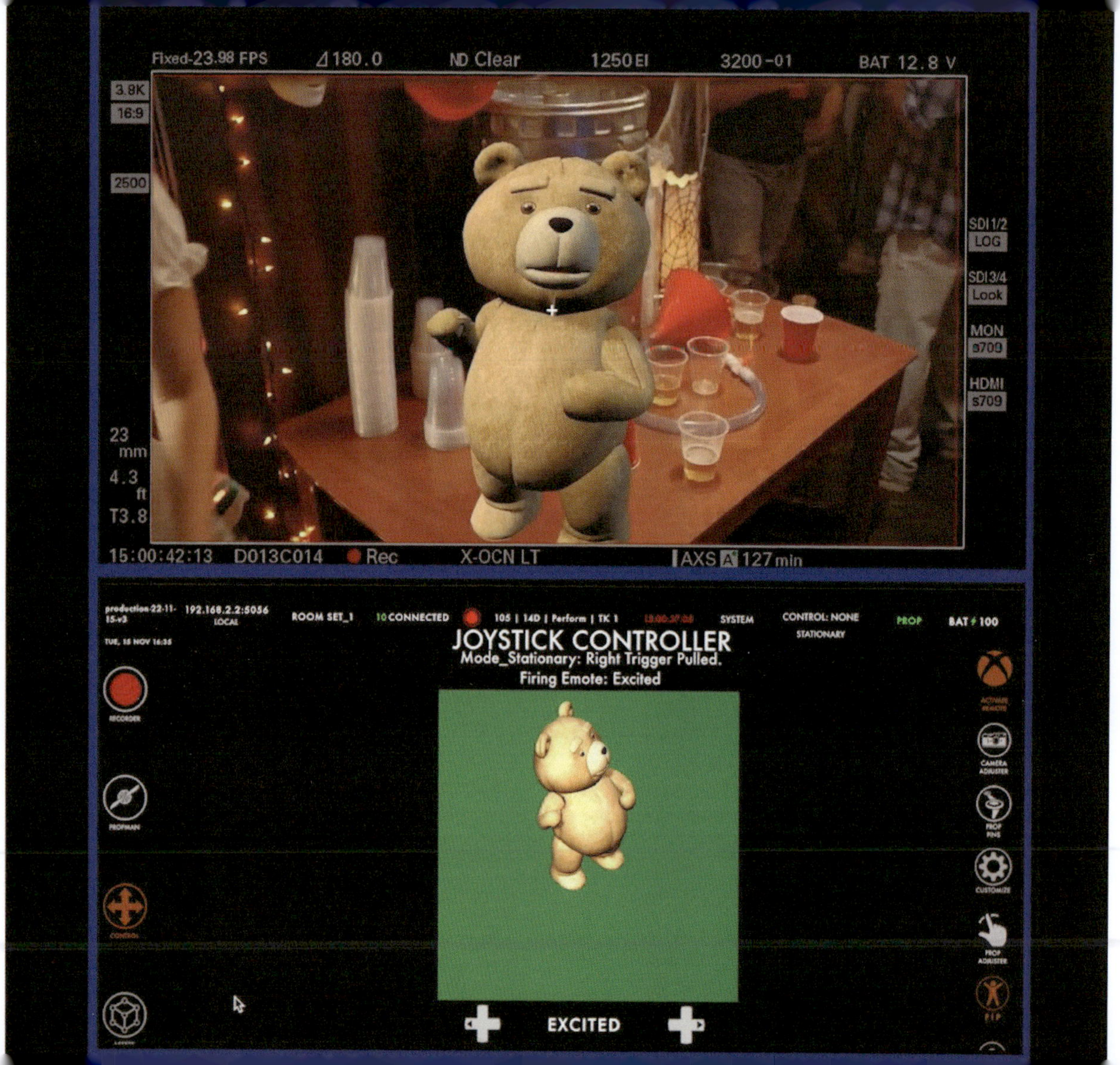

Fixed-23.98 FPS
⊿180.0
ND Clear
1250 EI
3200-01
BAT 12.8 V
3.8K
16:9
2500
SDI 1/2
LOG
SDI 3/4
Look
MON
s709
HDMI
s709
23 mm
4.3 ft
T3.8
15:00:42:13
D013C014
Rec
X-OCN LT
AXS A 127 min
production-22-11-15-v3
192.168.2.2:5056
LOCAL
ROOM SET_1
10 CONNECTED
105 | 14D | Perform | TK 1
SYSTEM
CONTROL: NONE
STATIONARY
PROP
BAT 100
JOYSTICK CONTROLLER
Mode_Stationary: Right Trigger Pulled.
Firing Emote: Excited
RECORDER
CAMERA ADJUSTER
CUSTOMIZE
PROP ADJUSTER
EXCITED

Blair Clark: It started the same and Seth quickly realized that because the cast was much bigger, and a lot of other things, and just trying to do a performance, then direct, and look at the scene–all that stuff happening at the same time was just, you couldn't do it. So, we abandoned the motion capture through production and it turned into a post thing. That put even more emphasis on what Brandon could do with ViewScreen so that we could still employ that through photography.

Brandon Fayette: He did it through the middle of a break, too. So, all of a sudden we went from a bear that was moving in ViewScreen with mo-cap to a bear that was completely static with a dead doll, so then we started adapting. We adapted puppeteering systems via game controllers and a markerless mo-cap system to do the head and facial performance, which was really just for reference so that we could see it. We'd do more high-fidelity captures in post. Blair would do the proper captures with the takes that they were recording in post after. But on the set we could see a living character, see it reacting and performing.

   It allowed us to build our system, which now can bring multiple sources of motion capture to any asset at any joint or shape. So we can have, for example, a situation where Seth would look down at his lines while he was performing Ted live, or he'd be looking at monitors in village while performing Ted and we're not getting an eye line from Ted to the characters. So we would turn off the head tracking, drive the head via puppeteer, and then we could still see in ViewScreen Ted reacting to the people around him but still get the facial performance. It's still Seth performing Ted, but the head is being driven entirely by someone live because he's obviously looking at all of his monitors and doing his own thing, but still performing. It was kind of a turn on, turn off, opt in, opt out version based on what the shot was of how we could build a performance that was still useful for the camera operators and the camera team to work with.

b&a: I'm also curious during, say, the shoot whether you relied on any pre-canned animation of Ted for a complex scene or even a non-complex scene?

Brandon Fayette: For the more complex scenes, ViewScreen wasn't able to do that. It's more specific to certain types of shots. Obviously the technology's evolved since *Ted*, so we can do more complex things than we started with. But we would bring in animations. There's times on set where I would animate something coming up and go to Blair, 'Hey, does this feel like how Ted would move?' And he'd be like, 'Do this a little bit, he walks a little more with a waddle like that.' And so, Blair and I would tweak some stuff and then apply it to the character.

   To give you a complex animation example, Seth is there performing, he's looking at the monitors directing, we're getting his facial performance via marker-less mo-cap to the bear. We're overriding the head because the shot is Ted walking alongside his best friend through a hallway. So we're using the walk cycles that Blair and I had gone back with to drive the walk of the bear, while moving the head with the puppeteer live while the face is being performed by Seth, so we could get a walk and talk shot, which is a pretty complex thing which you couldn't do with just Seth standing by himself. And even with the MVN suit, we weren't going to ever, I don't think, have him walk around to do those kind of things because there's too much locomotion.

Blair Clark: Yeah, it's like he wasn't tethered anymore, but still in a very constricted space. And then we would also do the same blocking with the stuffy pass because you still need that for the other actors so that they can get a sense of where he is through the blocking.

b&a: What did you find you had to overcome to enable useful things like getting occlusion to work?

Brandon Fayette: We started out at the beginning of *Ted* without occlusion, so we were running the system without him able to be occluded. If we're doing things like over the shoulder shots, Ted was always on top. We put in our own version of environment and human occlusion, the thing that's doing this right now live, into the system after the fact near the end of shooting. So, I think the last few episodes were when we started getting the occlusion system running because we had to roll our own from scratch, there wasn't anything that existed.

There's an iPhone side of ViewScreen that runs on i-devices, which is what we can use to puppeteer and control things. Apple has their own version of human occlusion on i-devices, but our system that put things into the camera operators' viewfinder is our own design. There were no human occlusion models, so we had to train our own networks to learn what a human was to put it in. Now we're at the point where we're not only doing human occlusion but we're doing depth sorting, so I could put someone inside of a vehicle behind the glass in between the steering wheel and the seat and put Ted in the car next to them and everybody's now sorted properly in 3D depth. But that wasn't something that existed during the filming of *Ted*.

There's lot of things that got created. I like to say that every time we were doing something on *Ted*, like when Seth decided he was not going to do the suit, we would pivot. And every pivot that we took never led to a dead end, it led to a new innovation and then we would take that and then build upon that. So, we were really fortunate that both with *The Orville*, but even more so with *Ted*, a lot of what we developed came out of that battle-tested system of, you're on set and weird things happen and things change and things go on the fly. Where we started at the beginning of filming *Ted* with the technology and where we ended up at the end of filming *Ted* was almost like a completely different tool set.

Blair Clark: What you showed me a couple of weeks ago was amazing. It was a completely different thing. The stuff that we can do now is just crazy compared to where we were on *Ted*.

Brandon Fayette: I mean, because Seth didn't want to wear the suit while filming, we worked on our own real-time full-body motion capture system. We're fully real time, so I can put a single phone and get a rough approximation of body across an entire shot live and stream it on a location scout, or even in the middle of shooting entirely in one sitting. So, the same thing that's driving the face that was moving Ted's head is now driving a full-body performance.

And it may not be as high fidelity as an Xsens suit or a solve from something like Move AI, but it's directable and it's live so you can get the broad strokes of it all and get what you need just to tell that story in the shot. And I also joke that what I have right now is I have the Holodeck in my pocket, so I can just pull it out and we can be inside of a full virtual environment and we're auto-keying people out and then that gets saved and sent across and it's all shared.

The big innovation for *Ted* versus *Orville*: On *Orville*, we were doing a couple cameras at a time, *Ted*, it was three cameras simultaneously, sometimes a fourth in waiting, and that was a big feed because you have to figure out how to synchronize all that to a time code and not break it.

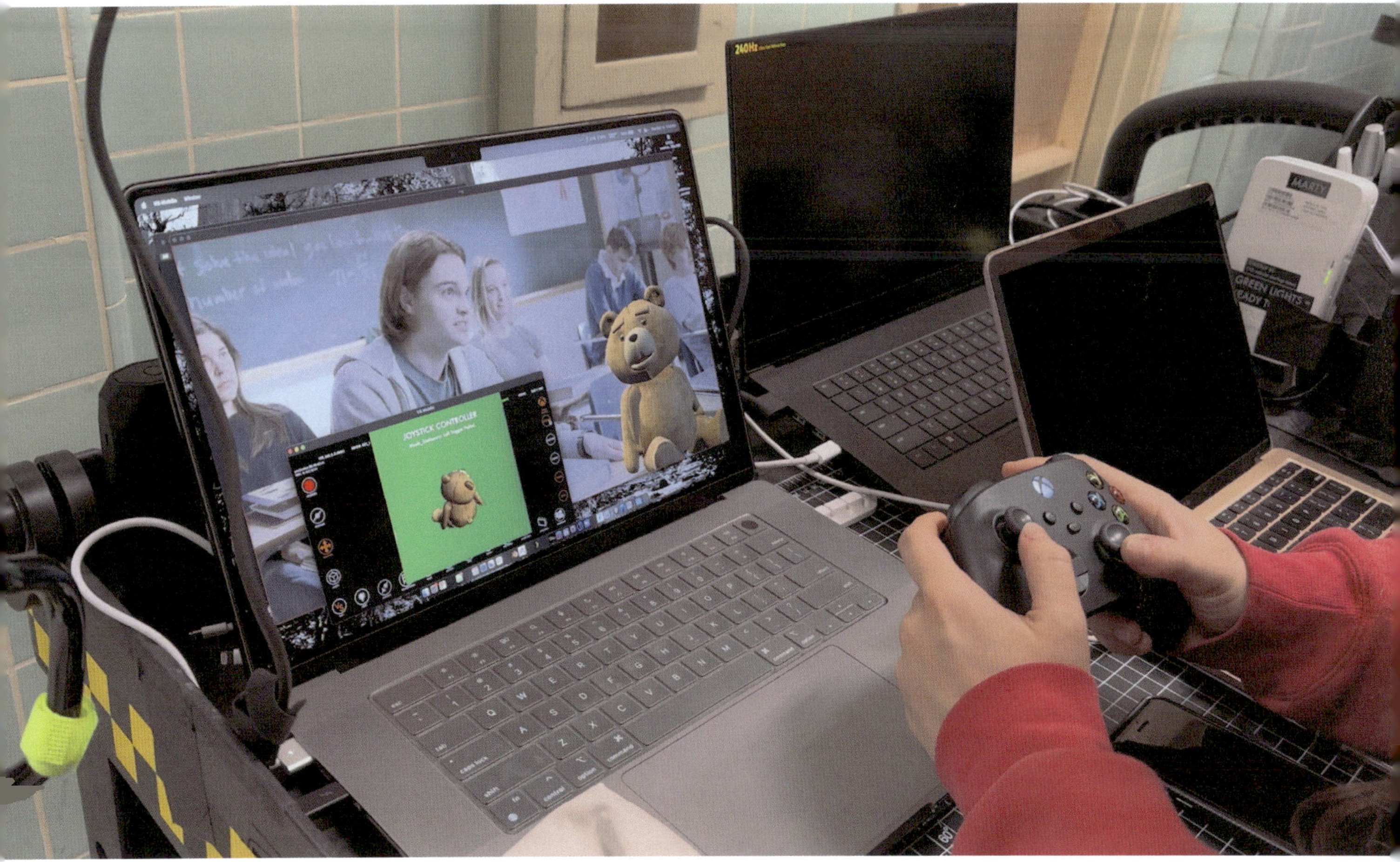
240Hz
JOYSTICK CONTROLLER

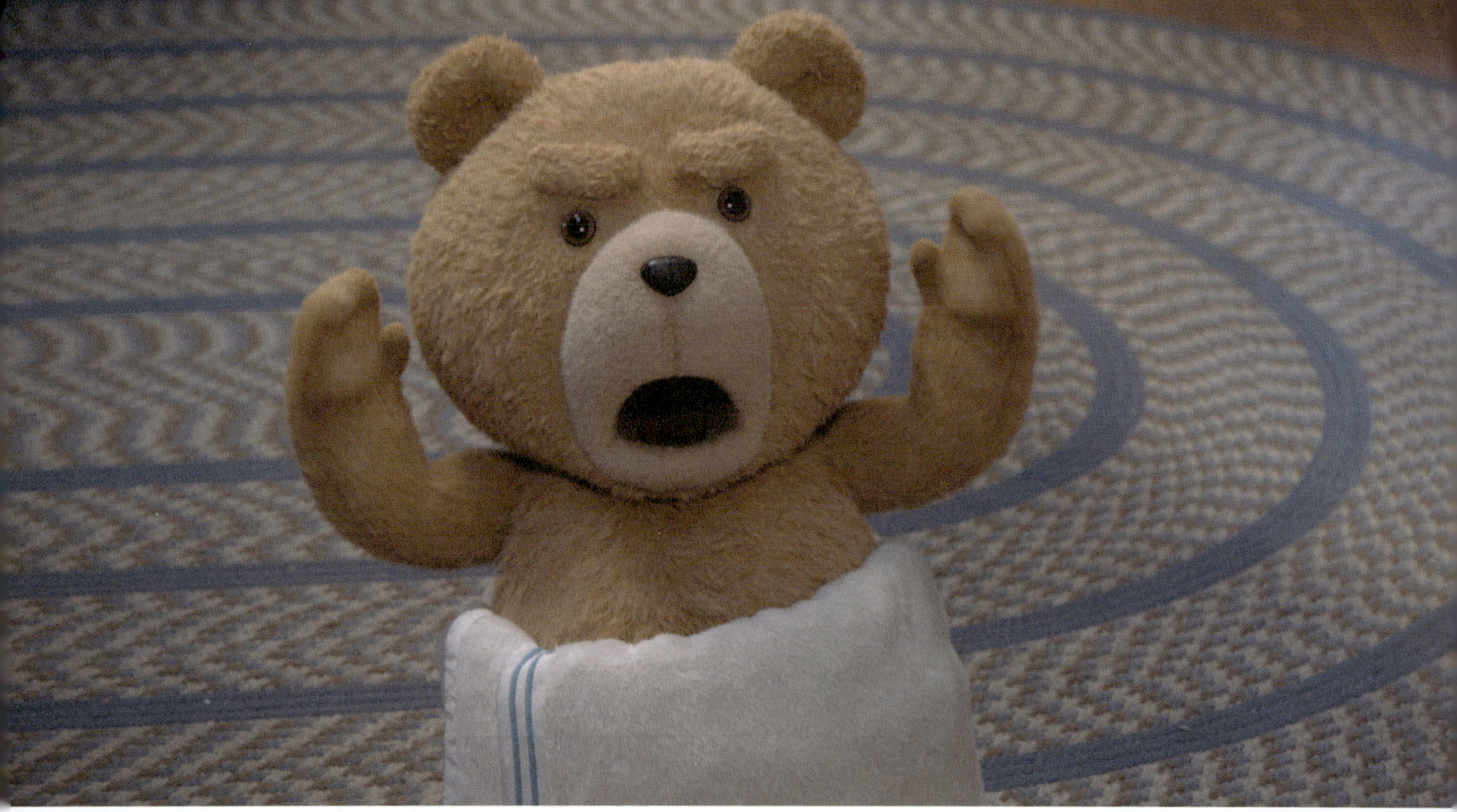

b&a: Blair, as a visual effects supervisor, this really gives the opportunity for not only your team, yourself and your team to see what it's going to look like, but it gives the camera operator the ability, the crew, the actors as well. What was that like on the series versus the feature films, but also other films and things you've done?

Blair Clark: Well, we didn't have anything like it before. So yeah, it's a really great tool that I'm looking forward to using on future shows.

Brandon Fayette: I owe Blair a lot, Blair was the most accommodating human being for us building this out and really tuning it on *Ted*. And if there was not a better partner to help work with me on this, it was Blair. I mean, he was always open to it and as we were building the pieces, he was like, 'Oh, this is kind of cool. Try that.' And it was just really nice to just have both of our brains there available. And obviously we also wanted to stay out of everyone's way. I think we did a pretty good job of that, Blair, of being pretty invisible on set. So that was another big key.

Blair Clark: Anybody that was aware of it certainly didn't take it as an impedance in any way.

Brandon Fayette: Yeah, which is important because you don't want to slow down the shoot. We always want to be able to augment things.

b&a: I feel like this clearly has a huge role in aiding the performance of the final character, but also the actors, a live action actor's performance. But one thing I've always marveled on, Blair, with the Ted films and now with the TV show is literally the integration of a CG character into the final shots. I just want to make sure to give yourself a shout-out, but also your team and the visual effects partners in doing that. What are the very traditional things you do, from stuffies to maybe color charts and other things that you do?

Blair Clark: It's all of that stuff. It was embracing ViewScreen and everything, but making sure that we didn't abandon the stuff that works so well and that some of these companies rely on. Definitely stuffies, definitely anything we can do on set to incorporate interaction with the physical world there. We always had the sticks with the balls on the end that we would punch people with. Anything like that to get any kind of interactivity, you always benefit from that so much.

And then just in post all the companies, Tippett Studio and Framestore working on the Ted character, and then we had Fuse doing the Dennis the Truck character, which is in one episode. They all did such a great job of finding things that they could do to incorporate him and integrate him into the scene.

b&a: I assume doing this process with ViewScreen gives you a kind of post-vis to use in the edit directly as opposed to just blank plates. Was that something that came into play a lot with Ted here?

Brandon Fayette: With *Ted*, we started to do a little bit of export that was used for reference. We exported out everything we did that was available for the editors to use. The data that we exported was also available for the VFX vendors, and we were designing it a little bit as we were going. So, there are certain shots I think where they used a little bit of it, certain shots that didn't. Right now we're able to do full Avid MXF exports of anything non-destructively with alpha channels as well as ProRes 4444. And we also export LIDAR data, scan meshes, EXR lighting passes, there are sphericals that come from the environment, and so on. But for *Ted*, it was a dealer's choice. We would do our dailies the same as everyone else, and we put it in a pot and let them use it what they needed.

Blair Clark: That kind of goes hand in hand with what I was talking about earlier about when you do a stuffy pass, you've always got the meathead holding the puppet who they have to go in and kind of try and clean it out as best possible. In screenings for the studio or for executives, they want to see stuff as soon as there's an assembly of it, and we never have anywhere near finished shots at that point, so the editorial team does the best they can with what they have. But now with this stuff that Brandon can export, it's a much cleaner representation of the character that they can put in.
b&a

Page 50: A driving scene for the Ted series is filmed, with ViewScreen used to visualize a digital Ted character as one of the passengers.

Page 53: The ViewScreen user interface.

Page 54: A virtual Ted was able to be animated during a scene with simple joystick controls.

Page 57: The joystick control and live comp abilities of ViewScreen on show.

Pages 58 & 61: Final shots by Framestore.

All images © 2023 Peacock TV LLC. All Rights Reserved.

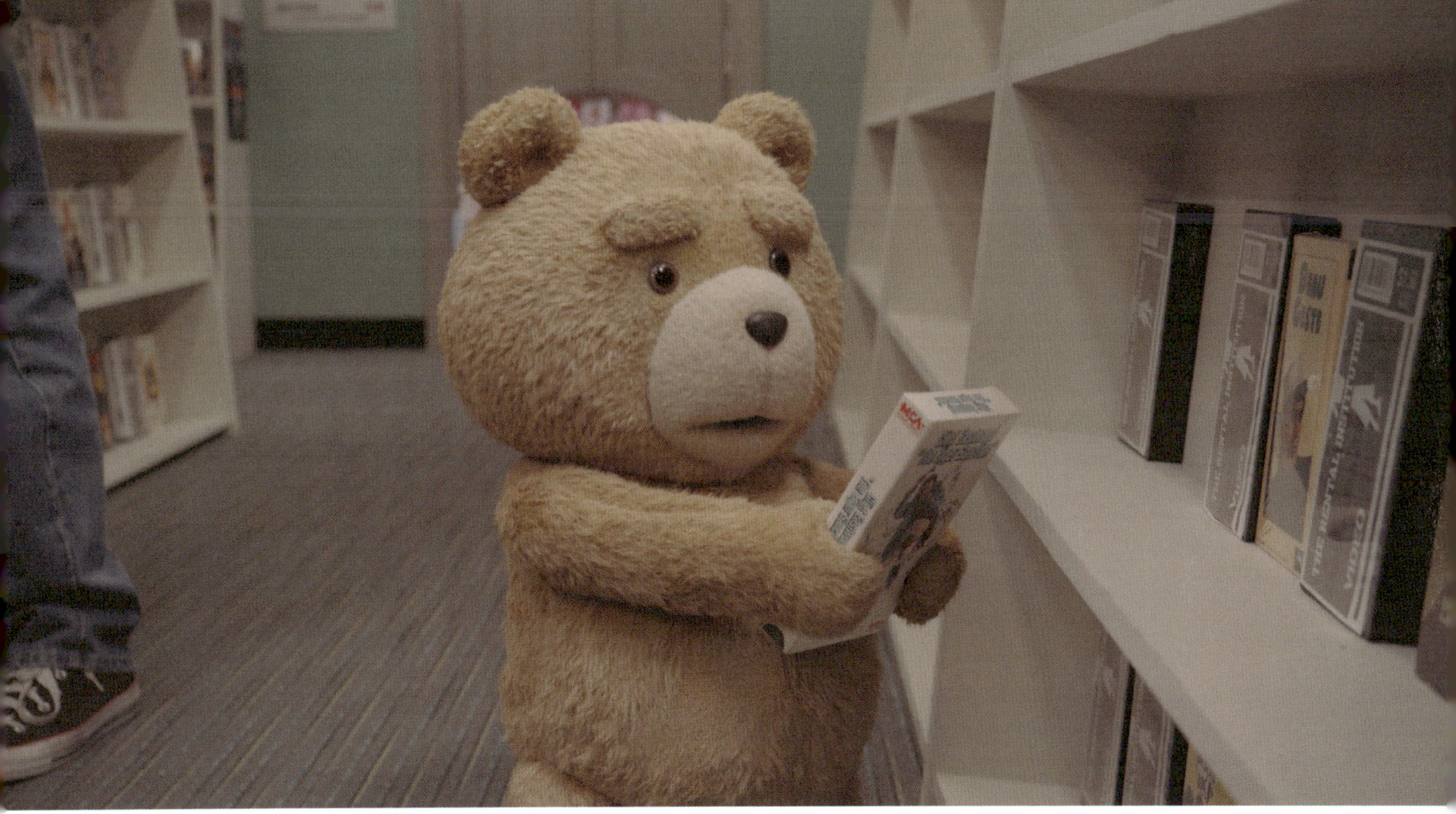

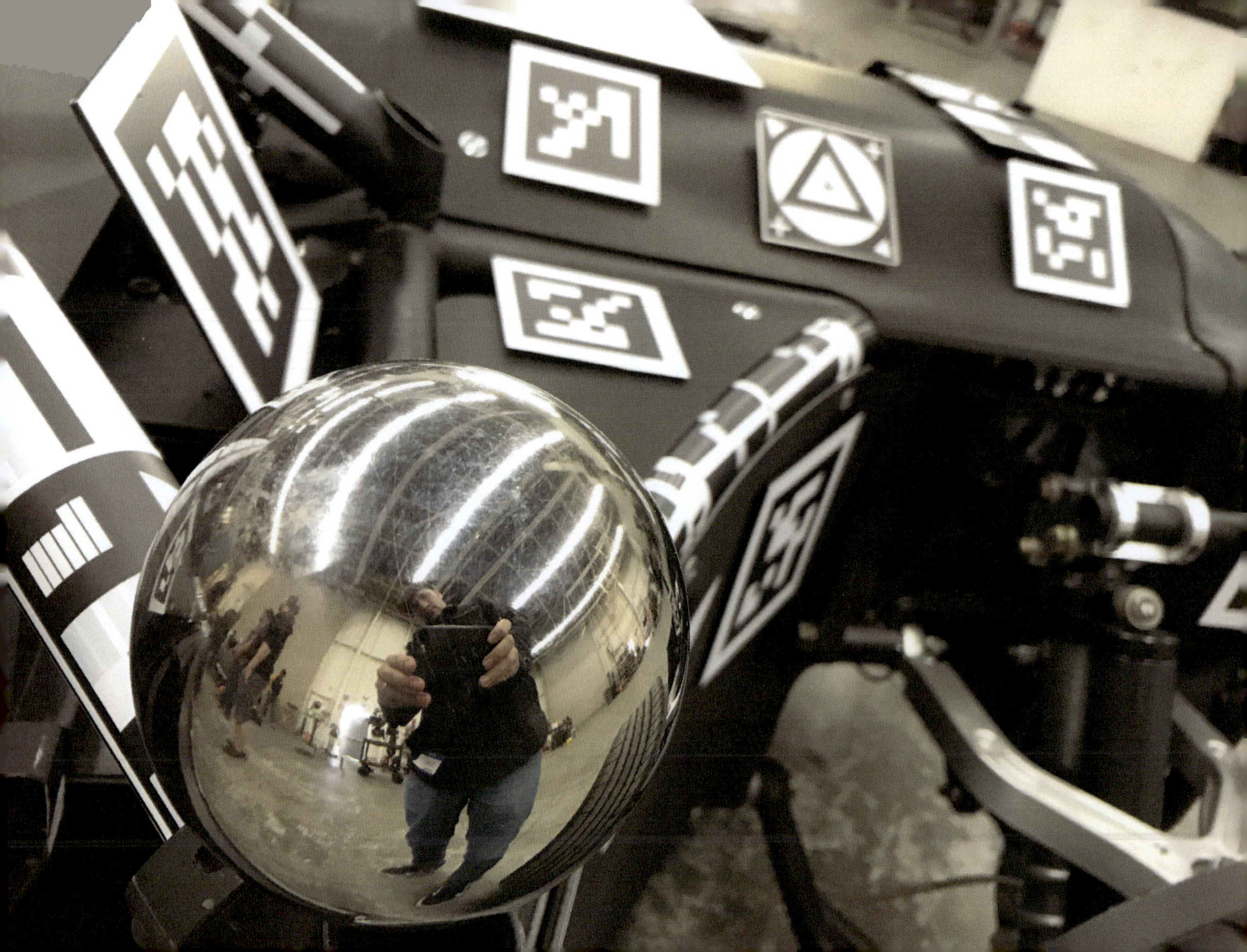

VIRTUAL PRODUCTION: A STATE OF PLAY WITH JIM GEDULDICK

A look back—and forward—at where we're up to in VP.
By Ian Failes.

Virtual production seemed to explode onto our screens in a frenzy via rapid innovations in real-time rendering, the use of game engines in filmmaking, and the making of *The Mandalorian*. While LED walls and the 'volume' are now the most commonly thought of uses of virtual production, the field also covers so many other aspects, including previs, techvis, VR scouting and motion capture.

Someone who has been fully immersed in the world of virtual production since the beginning—and who has a long history with cinematography and visual effects—is VFX supervisor and virtual production supervisor Jim Geduldick. Recently, he's worked on projects such as *Pinocchio*, *Masters of the Air*, *Yo Gabba GabbaLand* and *Here*, all in virtual production capacities.

That makes him well-placed to comment on the state of the virtual production industry, an industry that might be considered still in its early days, even if some of the technology and approach to the artistry has been around for some time.

In this Q&A, extracted from a recent longer *befores & afters* podcast episode, we delve into Geduldick's thoughts on where things are 'up to' right now with virtual production, and what the future of VP might be.

b&a: I always think it's an incredibly natural progression for someone who's good with camera and VFX to go into virtual production, which involves real-time, LED walls and lots of other things. The skills that you already have are completely relevant to this new world. It's actually very natural, right?

Jim Geduldick: Yeah, and there are the gaps in moving from one part of this industry into the other. If you were in games and then you moved into virtual production, you might have a really strong understanding of game engines in real-time. And then if you're moving from physical production and traditional VFX like comp but maybe weren't as familiar with the game engine side of things or media server side of things, then that's another way in.

For me as a VFX and a VP supervisor, it's all about, how am I interfacing with all these other people? How do I interpret and break things down for those other team members that may have not been part of this already? So, you're part interpreter, you're part technology breakdown person. I tend to make a beeline for the camera team. It's really easy for me to be like, 'Okay, what are your show specs, camera and lens choices? I'll tell you what we can deliver to you or what I need to get back from you.'

b&a: It's funny, too, because these days virtual production means so many things, doesn't it?

Jim Geduldick: Yes, we bring up all those different forms of it between previs and simul-cam and mocap and p-cap and all the viz's. But we all know virtual production when it gets put into a project for a segment or for the whole show, it *is* production. You have all your traditional roles that are now interfacing with all of these newer roles or roles that have similar counterparts. You might have someone that's a lighting TD and that person may have lots of meetings and interface with the DP, the gaffer, the key grip, the rigging team—all about where to physically put a production film light, and then how does that relate to the virtual film light?

The tent pole [for virtual production] always goes back to *The Mandalorian*. I'm really thankful that there was a beacon out there at first to go, hey, here's the technology and here's how these different sides of production have come together. It's basically rear and front projection, and LEDs. They've been used for a very long time. Projection techniques go way, way back. We're talking well over 50 years in terms of the early days of what would be even deemed virtual production.

I do think there's technologies within virtual production that are new, that have brought the medium into the future a bit more, and to where we are today and where we'll be in the coming years. But I think the adoption was like a really big boom over COVID, and it let people see the different parts of virtual production.

b&a: One of the things that I think has evolved since *The Mandalorian* showcased LED wall volume virtual production is this concept of final pixel in-camera VFX. Early on it just seemed to me almost like a 'boasting' point was how much you could film on an LED wall and capture something final pixel or in-camera. It seems like it's evolved a little bit where the goal now is, instead, sometimes just to immerse the crew, the actors, into some kind of representation of the scene, or the goal is to have great use of the LED for on-set lighting and interaction. Have you noticed that evolution in terms of why we're even doing LED wall volume filmmaking and what it's good for?

Jim Geduldick: Sometimes you intend for a shot or a sequence to be final pixel and hopefully you have done your pre-light, your tech days and all of that to find out much earlier [that it won't be final pixel] than to go have all these lavish sets and very still expensive LED volumes set up. And it does happen. And it can happen for reasons of creativity. You don't ever want these tools to be restrictive to your other creative partners in the project. You don't want to be able to tell a cinematographer, 'Hey, no, you can't do that because of X, Y or Z.' You want to explain the technical reasons or the creative impact of, 'Hey, if you do this, it could break camera tracking.'

You may have a shot where it's being shot on the volume, but the plan right from the get-up might be that it goes through a traditional comp pipeline and you may use the benefit of having that particular shot on a volume because the time it will save you for using the image-based lighting part of an LED volume outweighs what you know you're going to have to do to potentially touch up that shot.

There's a lot of reasons why [you wouldn't be able to do something final pixel]. It could be something somebody picks up in dailies that somebody didn't pick up on set, which might be like, 'Oh, you hit this moiré threshold because you got the camera too close to the wall.' Or the pixel pitch of the wall maybe wasn't a really fine one like a

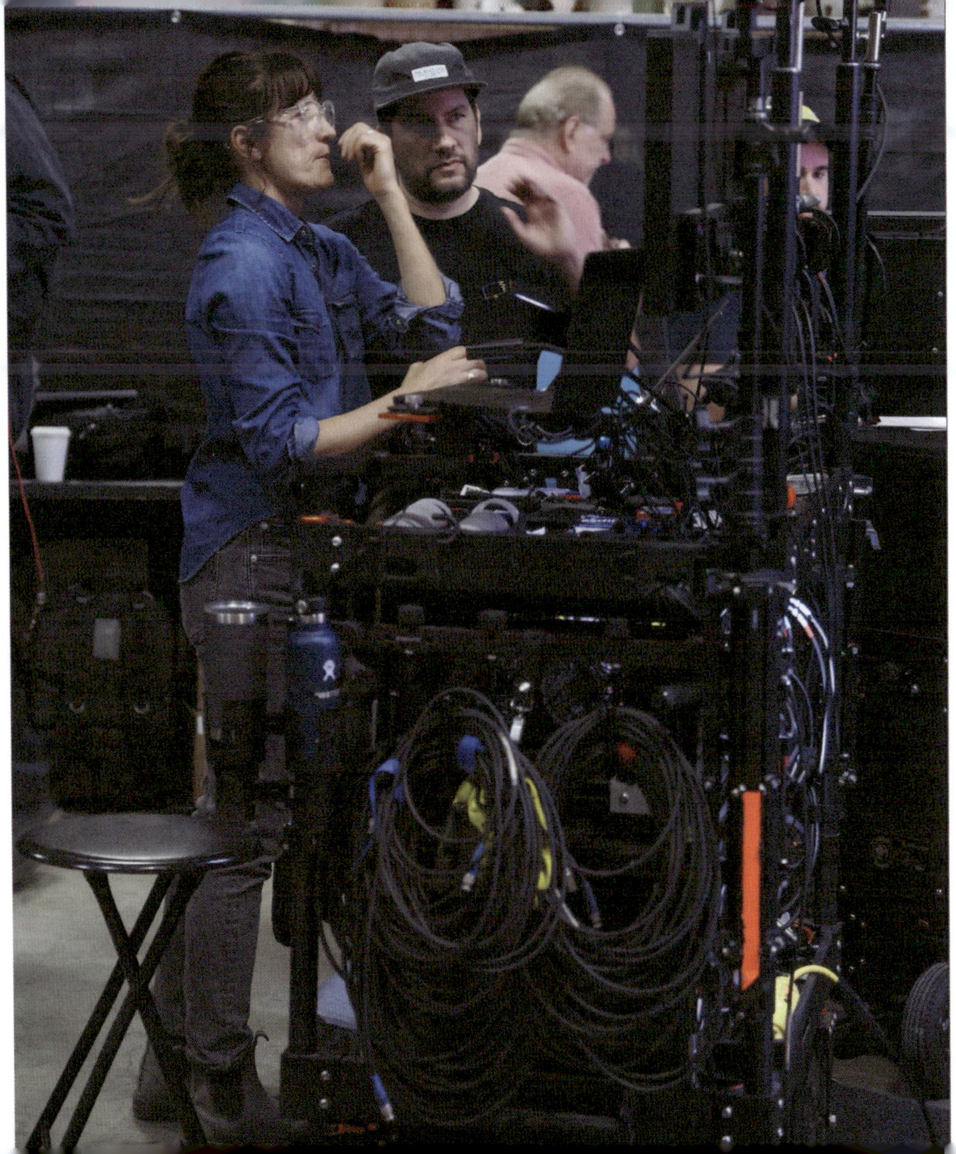

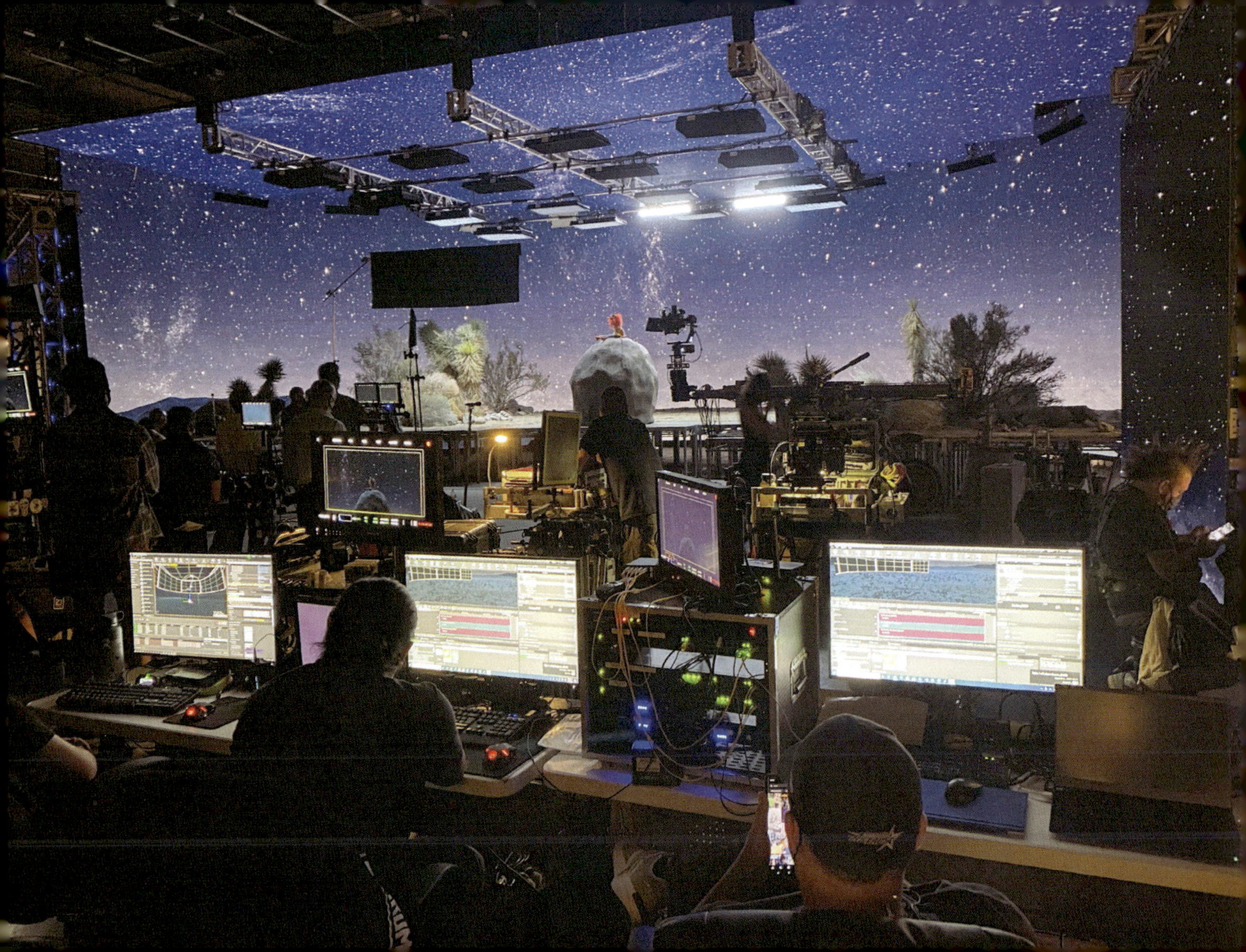

1.9, maybe you're on a 2.8. It happens. Maybe that shot might need to be touched up. It might have to go through roto and paint. That does happen. I wouldn't be trying to sugarcoat anything to be like, 'Oh, well, we always get it in the can.' No, we hit problems just like any other traditional production workflow.

But I would say the other side of that is there's definitely been shots and sequences and entire episodes that I have worked on where you would do your traditional DI but you might not need to touch up any of the ICVFX plates, because they happen to just work. I will say a lot of that takes your previs and your tech planning and your pre-light days and your tech days. And I think, speaking to any supes out there, we really do try to fight for those prep days because, even if you're on a traditional shoot, getting those extra days to plan and prep and step through and audition things ahead of time is always something we're always fighting for.

b&a: How hard is it to get up to speed on some of the new things in virtual production and to keep up with developments?

Jim Geduldick: It's daunting. I won't lie. It is daunting to stay on top of the changes. Staying on top of the panels or the color science alone, can confuse a lot of people. You've got decisions on pixel pitch on panels, you've got the color rendition of the panels, you've got the color rendition and the color science of the imaging sensor and the lenses that you're working with. It's not something you can learn off a YouTube video. You have to be hands on with this stuff and you have to be working on the volume. The more you hone your skills, the quicker you can have a better understanding of it.

And when things break, because they do, you know how to adapt to that thing breaking really quick. So if you're in-engine and you're operating and the lighting is breaking, well, where do you go? If you are not the sole vendor, not the virtual art department, then you may have a different stage operation team, and you are not the end to end solution, you really have to have a good pipeline. Or, if you're the overall supervisor then you have to make sure that you have everybody delivering hopefully on time to get the assets.

b&a: Because virtual production is so new, it keeps changing in the way that it interacts with VFX and animation and filmmaking. Where do you see the immediate future of it? Obviously on the tip of everyone's tongue is machine learning and AI right now.

Jim Geduldick: We all know that AI is the hot button topic. I mean, can you slim down a team because of this one platform that's promising that you could do roto faster? Or, with text to 3D, does that mean you would get assets quicker? You look at everything, from how we're using NeRFs and gaussian splats that have skyrocketed in their potential use case on an LED volume as a background, because we have more of a free view camera that we can frame and position. And if you can go out and capture with a high fidelity system set—you've got LiDAR, you've got photogrammetry, you've got digital cinema cameras, and you've got camera arrays that we build—and we go out and we shoot and it needs to be a photoreal project, well, two years ago, what we were first talking about NeRFs, it's a thousand light years ahead of what it was.

I'm a fan, I'm a user, I have been using all these modalities of computer vision and machine learning. A lot of the generative content has a lot of potential. But there's also a lot of unanswered questions with AI as a whole. We don't fully know where the data is coming from that a lot of the training is happening on. I'm cautious or have been cautious of our use of it—because we have been using it in a lot of different projects—but it's all about where it slots in, in the pipeline.

Right now, a lot of the generative models in virtual production use cases are, well, they have a hard stop at a point. They legally may not be able to be used because there is no copyright and IP ownership to the content that you would create as a hired vendor for a studio, for a brand, for an agency, or even for a music video. We know a lot of these companies have scraped their data and continue to scrape their data and it gets used. That being said, we have been training our own datasets with open source tools and custom tools.

It's really exciting right now because every other day there's a new model that comes out. But if you understand how they work in a pipeline, they're not one click solutions. So when I look at these things and where they slot in, I say, well, how can this help a VAD team? How can this help me on set? How can this help me work faster with the team to deliver something?

The NeRFs and the G-splats and the generative models—they aren't final pixel quality yet. Your assets will still need to get touched by a technician or an artist to get it to be final pixel. Can you get a high mesh poly model just by typing in a prompt? Sure. Is it usable? That's questionable. Does it still need to go into ZBrush and Marvelous Designer and all the other tools that do it? Yeah, it's still being done that way. Digital humans is another thing. But maybe one day we won't need 136 cameras to shoot digital twins. It might be a lot less because of synthesized data that can have a single point of capture that could capture all the information.

Right now, one of the best use cases for these newer models is in previs, techvis and concept design. That doesn't mean I want to go out and get rid of a talented storyboard artist or a concept designer or a matte painter. In some areas, these tools can be really assistive. Technology has always shown that it's going to shake things up. Film has always used technology to enhance story, and especially in visual effects. We've always done that. We've always been breaking the mold and trying to develop new things. **b&a**

Page 62: Jim Geduldick surveys The Mill's Blackbird car used to craft a virtual production dubbed 'The Human Race', from Epic Games, The Mill and Chevrolet. Image courtesy Jim Geduldick.

Page 65: Geduldick confers on the set of a production with DP Jac Fitzgerald. Image courtesy Jim Geduldick.

Page 66: Behind the scenes of the production of The Muppets Mayhem, on which Geduldick was a virtual production supervisor at Dimension Studio.

Page 69: A still from Yo Gabba GabbaLand!. © 2024 Apple TV+.

69

70

BREAKING DOWN A VIRTUAL PRODUCTION SHOOT

In this special visual story, filmmakers **Habib Zargarpour** *and* **Setareh Samandari** *give befores & afters a unique insight into their virtual production shoot for an upcoming documentary. Certain scenes required a number of virtual sets. For those, the production shot on greenscreen and relied upon simul-cam setups to realize live on-set composites.*

Page 70: Virtual production supervisor Habib Zargarpour on the set of a documentary recreation applying a simul-cam virtual production process involving accurate camera tracking and lens mapping with Mo-Sys and the Unity game engine. The director Nauzanin Knight and first DP Eric Spoeth are seen in the real-time comp [insert picture] of a virtual library discussing the next shot.

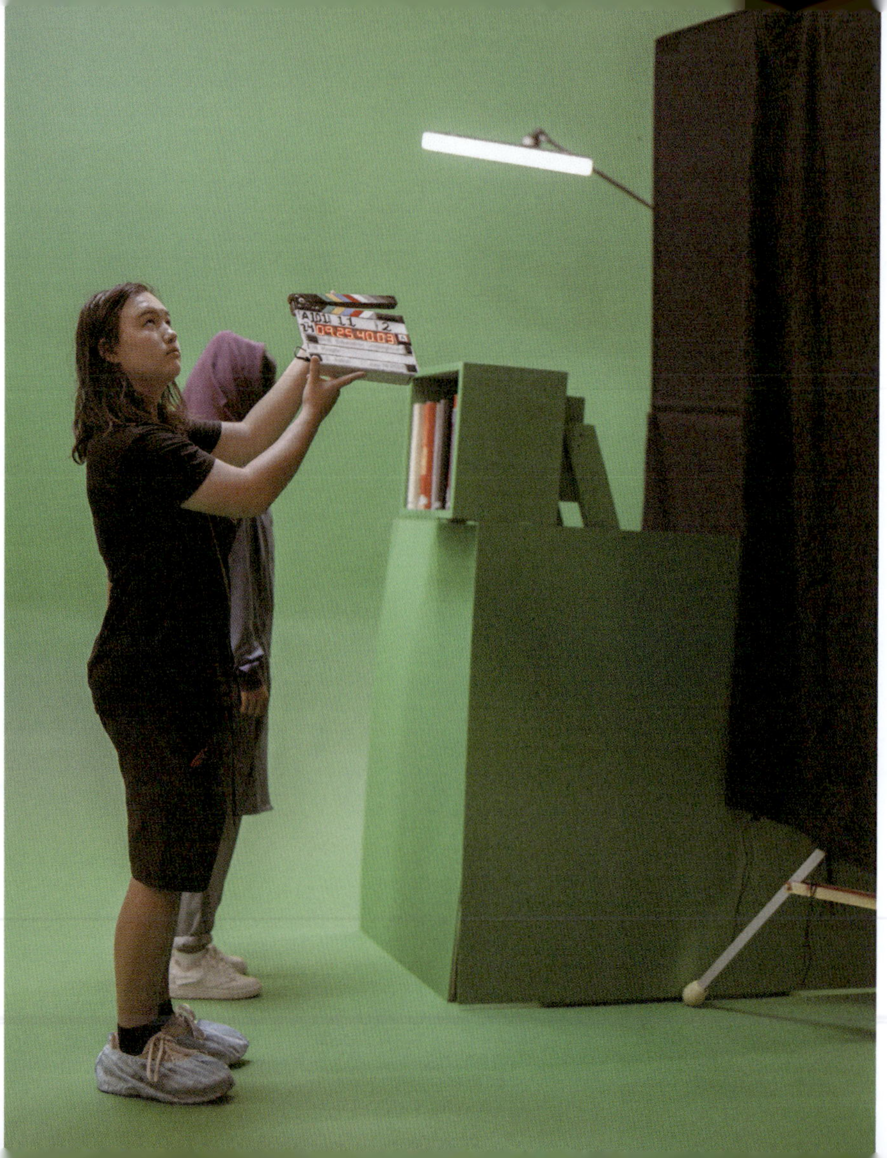

Page 72: Physical set for the library for actors to interact with real books while the rest is all generated and comp'd in real-time. The director and DP could see the shot compositions, make adjustments to the virtual set orientation and prop placement in real-time. The DP Chase Gardiner would control the camera head remotely while looking at the real-time comp.

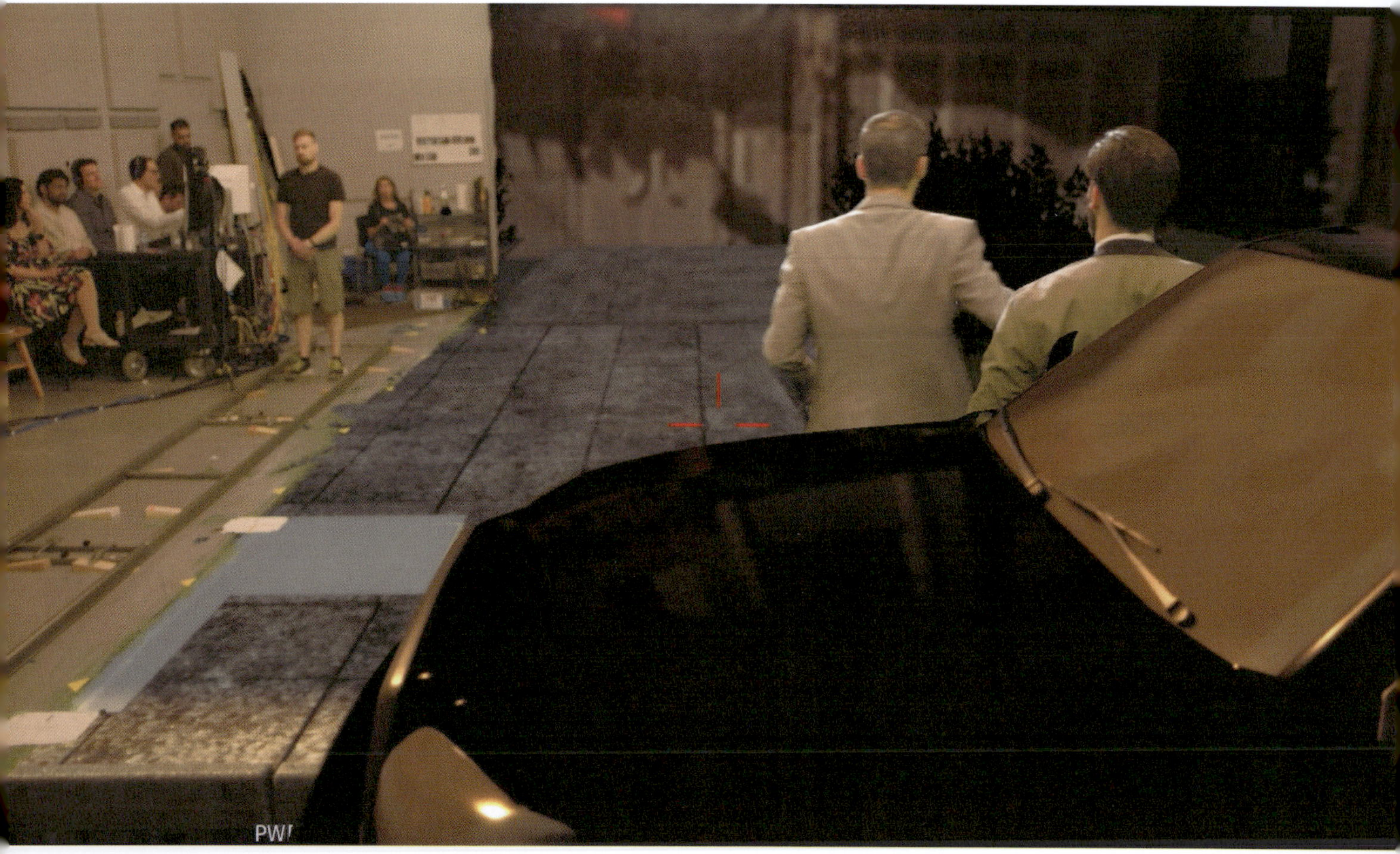

Page 74: A live simul-cam comp showing actors getting out of an SUV. The added capabilities on-set were written by Sergi Valls Company which built a plugin to add foreground mattes in real-time based on depth. In this case the SUV was comp'd on top of the actors. The shot starts low to the ground focused on the wheel as the car arrives, then booms up to reveal the actors getting out. The system was set up with time code and genlock working across the camera, Mo-Sys' StarTracker, Blackmagic Design's Ultimatte 12G and the PC running Unity with a Blackmagic DeckLink.

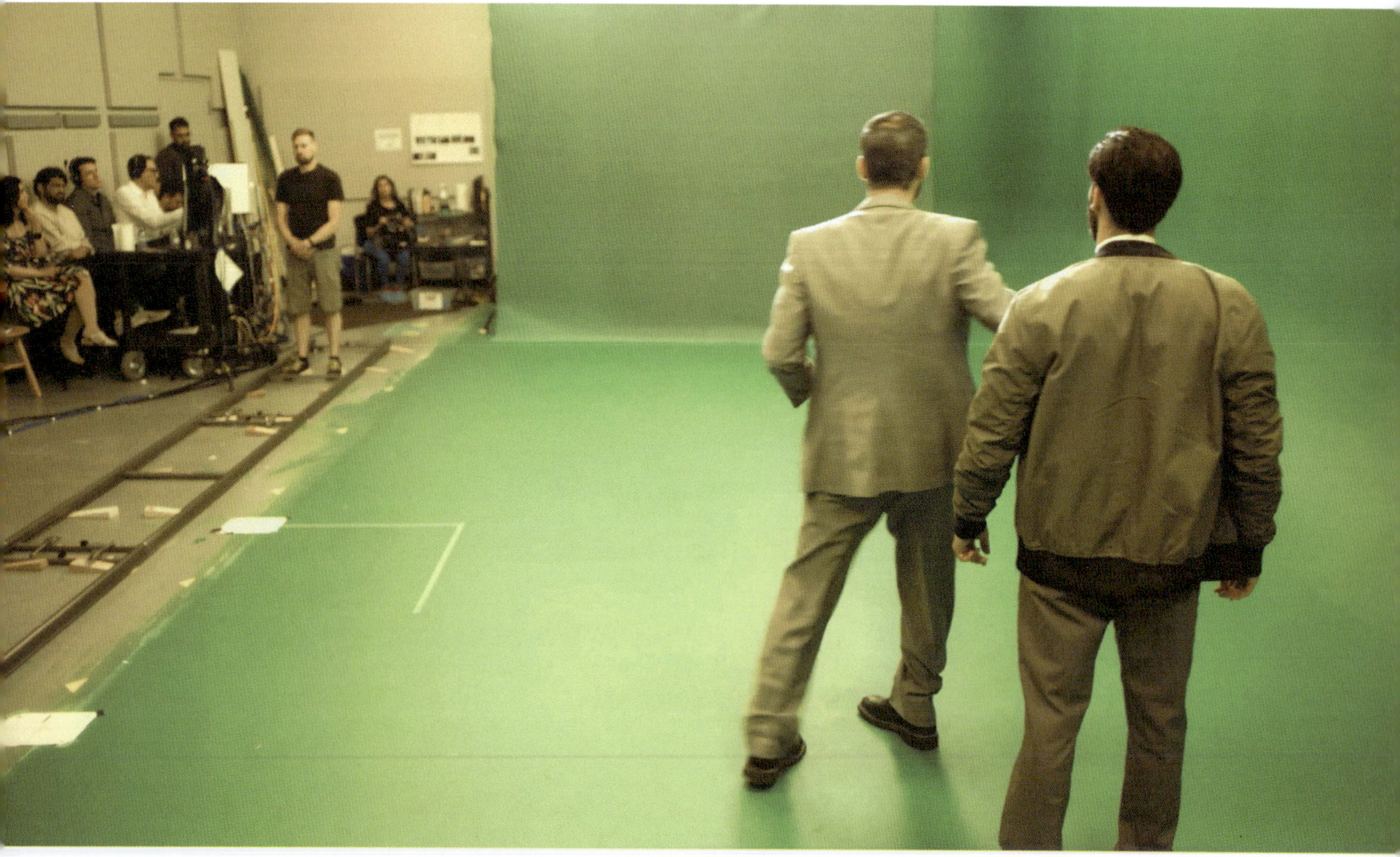

Page 76: This frame show what the camera saw in the SUV shot with only a green apple box (off screen) for the actors to step down from. The Dolly for the 20' Boom arm can be seen on the left. The ability to align the for camera to virtual elements was extremely helpful for the shots to be composed properly. The Mo-Sys camera tracking eliminated the need for extra greenscreen markers and expensive tracking in post. The virtual origin can be seen as one of the two sheets of paper on the edge of the greenscreen.

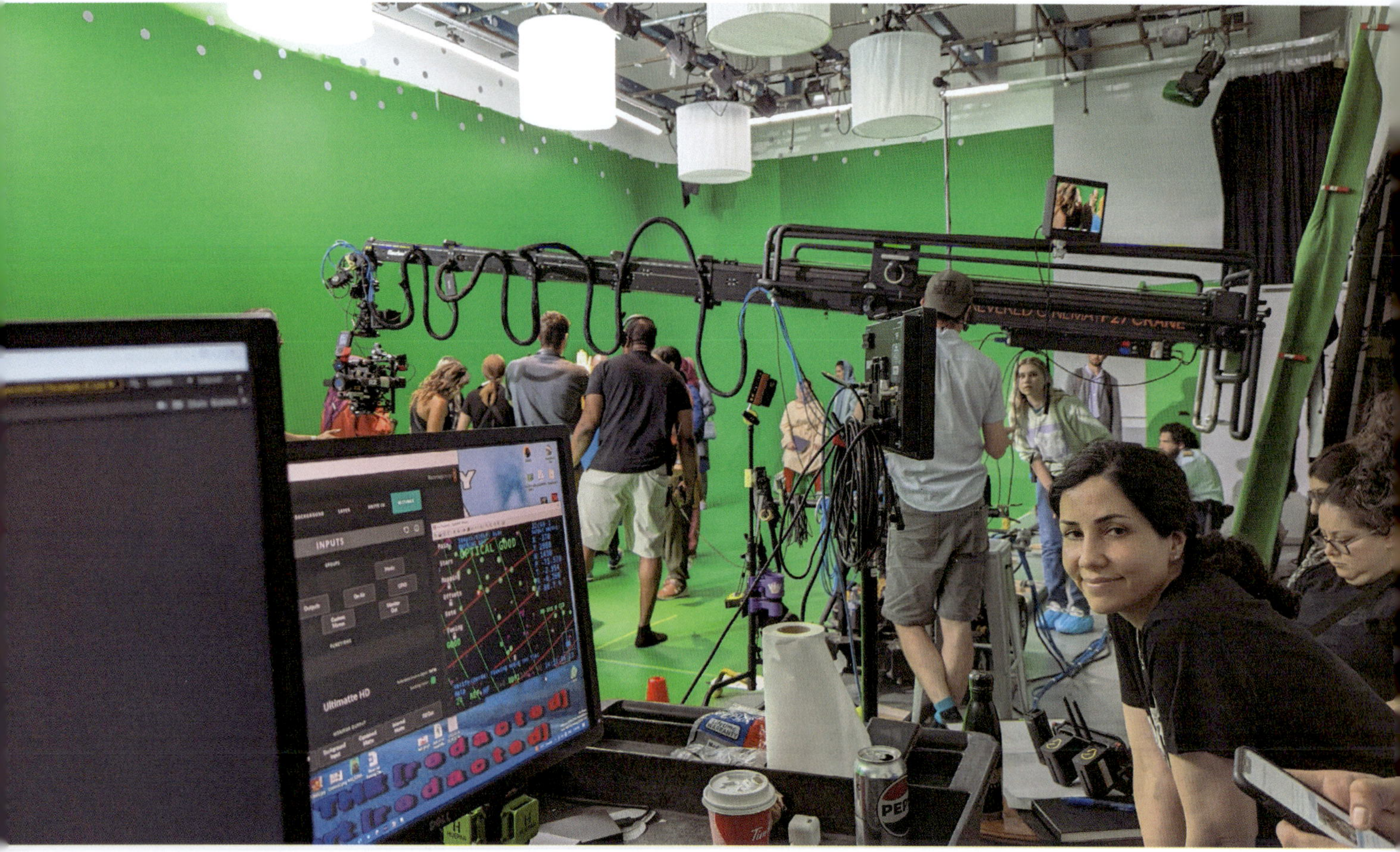

Page 78: Associate visual effects supervisor Setareh Samandari overseeing the greenscreen and wardrobe to ensure that the keying process in post will go as smoothly as possible.

Page 80: Habib Zargarpour and Setareh Samandari discussing the lighting match between the real and virtual sets, something that was adjusted live between them and the DP. Sometimes the lighting was driven by the virtual set, and sometimes the lighting on the real set would establish the direction. All the scenes had been previsualized in the virtual sets prior to the shoot and the same content was detailed out for the live shoot.

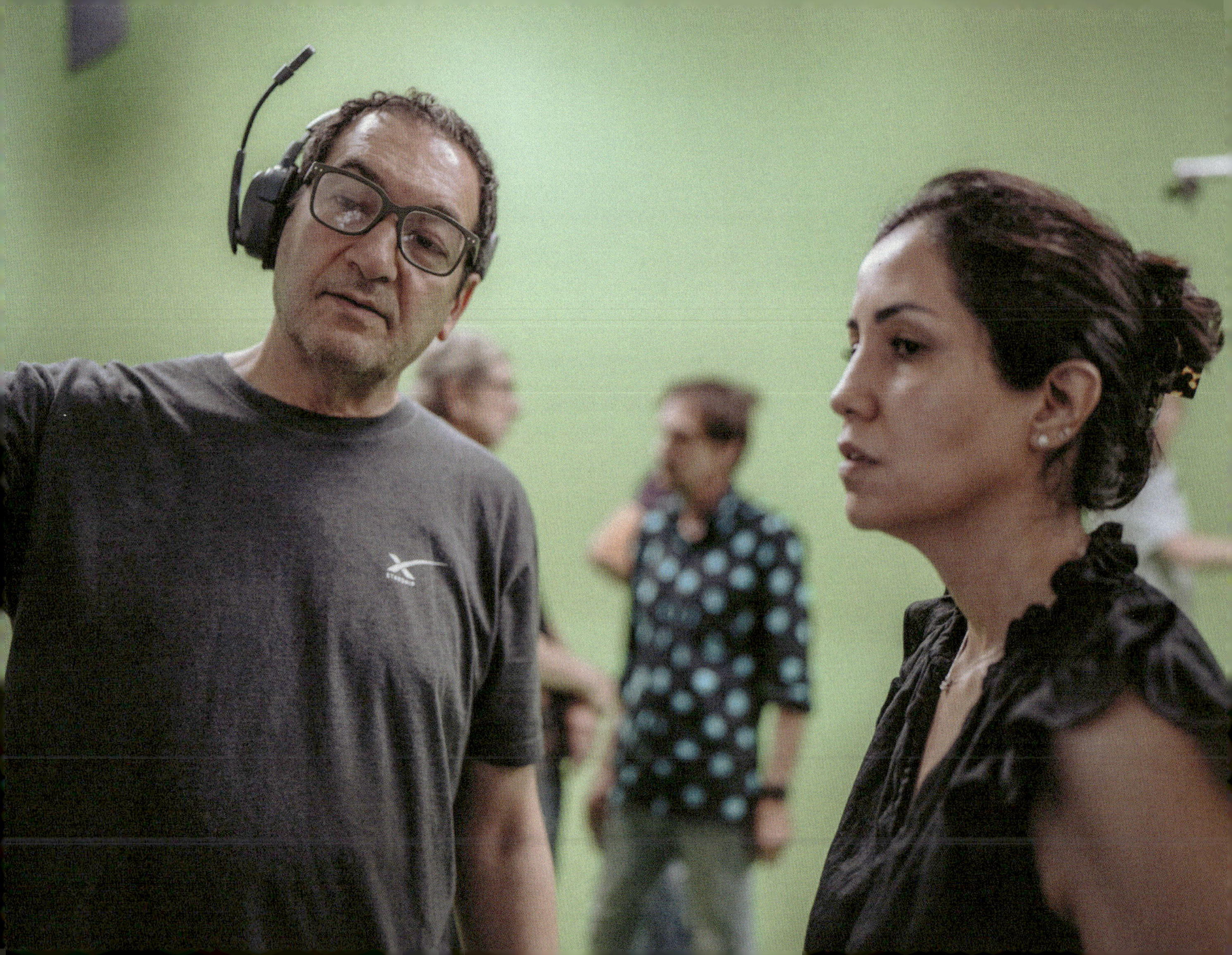

Printed in Great Britain
by Amazon